The Craft of Pottery

The Craft of Pottery

*A problem-solving approach to the
fundamentals of pottery making*

Frank Howell

Carol Woodward

Robert H. Woodward

HARPER & ROW, PUBLISHERS

New York, Hagerstown, San Francisco, London

Designed by Lydia Link

Title page photograph by Neil Scholl
Pottery (left to right): casserole by Jay Trenchard, planter by Frank Howell, vase by Dave Burnham, bowl by Judy Howell, bean pot by Frank Howell

---

Library of Congress Cataloging in Publication Data

Howell, Frank, 1940–
  The craft of pottery.
  Bibliography: p.
  Includes index.
  1. Pottery craft.   I.   Woodward, Carol, 1927–
joint author. II.   Woodward, Robert Hanson, 1925–
joint author. III. Title.
TT920.H69 1975   738   74–15859
ISBN 0–06–011966–7
ISBN 0–06–011959–4 pbk.

---

77 78 79 80 81 10 9 8 7 6 5 4 3 2 1

For Judy, Larry, and Bill

Contents

Preface

Pottery making can be treated as a simple craft or as a complex and technical art. It can be practiced with satisfaction by a child working at a school bench or by a home hobbyist at a kitchen table, making small pinch pots or coiled or slab forms with only his hands and the simplest of tools, and completing his creations with prepared glazes fired in a small kiln that will fit any table top. At its highest levels, it draws on chemistry in the compounding of clays and glazes, on physics in the design and construction of kilns, on mechanics in the fabrication of pottery wheels and other machines useful to the potter, and on the subjectivity of artistic judgment. The bridge joining the simple craft and the complex art is a long one.

This book is written for the reader who is somewhere on that bridge, taking his first steps or approaching the farther end. We envision the reader to be a person who wants to know what pottery making is all about, or at least enough of what it is about to be able to make sturdy and well-designed pottery using the potter's wheel and the traditional methods of hand-building. We imagine the reader is a person of artistic bent who is interested in trying out different methods of pottery making, who wants to know enough about designing and decorating pottery to produce objects that are creatively satisfying, and who wants to learn enough of the technical aspects of pottery making—formulating glazes and operating a kiln—to be able to perform all of the processes of pottery making from start to finish.

This book, then, is for the beginner—but a beginner who can move, if he wishes, to the more complicated aspects of the potter's craft, using the basic processes and techniques that are discussed and illustrated in detail. The beginner we are speaking to is thus both the novice potter and the student who has yet to define himself as a professional potter.

We have tried to put together a practical book, one that moves in an orderly fashion through a series of steps and processes that often overlap confusingly. After two introductory chapters—which glance at pottery history and at clay, the material from which all pottery is made, and which explain the requirements for setting up a simple studio and the basic process of wedging clay and preparing it for use—we move to the process of throwing. Here we begin with "throwing off the mound," a technique that has psychological advantages for novice potters and also acquaints them with the method used by production potters who make large quantities of pots on the wheel.

The next two chapters deal with other techniques of making pottery on the wheel and with the traditional hand-building methods of pinching, coiling, and using slabs. Then follow a chapter on design, decoration, and glazing—discussing principles and procedures that apply to all pottery—and another chapter on combining techniques of construction and decoration to create pottery that touches the edge of sculpture. The book concludes with chapters explaining the essential technical features of pottery—firing kilns and formulating glazes—a final chapter discussing some of the aspects of becoming a professional potter, and a glossary defining all specialized terms used in the book.

Throughout the book we recognize the difficulties and intricacies of creating with clay, and we illustrate the basic processes fully, step by step, at the same time discussing the problems that are almost certain to occur and the ways of avoiding or solving these problems. To the practiced potter, clay is the easiest of substances to work with. To the novice, however, it can be a slippery—or sometimes a gummy—substance that seems alien to the human hand. Reputedly plastic, it seems sometimes to be wholly uncooperative, firmly opposed to doing what

it ought. But the problems it creates can be solved, and we have given attention to those problems and their solutions.

In addition to the problem-solving approach, several other features of the book are worth noting. We have closely coordinated written instructions in process sequences with the process photographs to minimize the difficulty of learning the often tedious but all-important basic processes and techniques. At the end of each of the three chapters on throwing, we have summarized the major processes so that they are conveniently available to the potter who is busy at the wheel, with clay-stained hands. We have avoided the temptation to combine a book of instruction with an exhibition catalog and have illustrated only finished pieces that can be made through the use of the techniques and processes we explain or illustrate. These pieces are discussed with respect to any special features of construction or decoration, so that they, too, are instructive as well as, we hope, pleasing to look at.

Unless noted below or in the accompanying captions, all of the pottery in the book was made by authors Frank Howell and Carol Woodward. The hands of the potter in the process sequences are Frank Howell's; the hands of the potter holding the camera belong to Carol Woodward, who also photographed most of the finished pieces of pottery in the volume. The words are a joint effort of all three authors.

We wish to express our special gratitude to Jay Trenchard for his technical advice and counsel, particularly in Chapters 9 and 10; to Bart Connally for processing most of the photographs and for technical assistance; to Professor Emeritus Warren W. Faus, San Jose State University, for reading part of the manuscript; and to Nahum Waxman and Susan Schnur of Harper & Row for their editorial assistance and encouragement. We thank several potters for permission to publish photographs of their work: Patricia Haeger, Judy Howell, Freeman Loughridge, Steve O'Loughlin, Judy Pitkin, Jay Trenchard, and Robert L. Wolchock. And we are grateful to the M. H. de Young Memorial Museum, San Francisco, and the Asian Art Museum of San Francisco, Avery Brundage Collection, as well as to several manufacturers, identified in captions, for furnishing photographs.

F.H., C.W., R.H.W.

The Potter's Craft

From out the molten earth emerged the rock
To face the seasons' change, the force of wind,
The pounding of the rain, the brutal shock
Of ice and fire, the grinding power that thinned
The rock away.
          The earth gave birth to grass
And trees, which thrived and died and in their death
Joined to the earth from which they sprang. That mass
Locked elements as clay.
             Then man gave breath,
And with his hands gave shape to shapeless clay
To serve his needs—his hunger, thirst, and eye.
His life had found its centered, opened way;
His spirit lifted up toward the sky.

    The potter's craft remains, its center sure—
    The potter and his pottery endure.

R.H.W.

The Craft of Pottery

Pottery and Clay

POTTERY: A GLANCE AT HISTORY

Pottery making is one of the most ancient of crafts, its origins found in the earliest periods of many cultures. Although the complete history of pottery can never be told, the first pottery was probably the work of some primitive artisan who learned that clay could be shaped easily by hand when it was moist and would retain its shape when it dried. The first clay wares were no doubt crude figures or utensils modeled after natural forms, such as gourds or even large leaves, known to hold seeds or grain. But dried clay is not impervious to the elements, and it melts back into mud in the rain. It was probably not for many ages after man first began to shape clay that he finally learned how to render it next to indestructible.

When clay is subjected to intense heat it undergoes a chemical and physical change that turns it into a stonelike material. Like stone, it does not easily wear away, but it can break. The first records of the craft of pottery are, therefore, pottery fragments, or shards, which have been found by archeologists across the face of the globe. This widespread distribution indicates that pottery cannot be said to have a single history, begun in one place at a single time. Rather, it has literally dozens of histories. Pottery emerged as cultures developed and as the requirements of life made necessary the utensils and objects required for the business of everyday living.

Most of the early output was predominantly practical in character. Drainage pipes and brick sewers were used in Central Asia and the Near East as long ago as 2500 B.C., and earthenware tiles and bricks, decorated with painted figures or glazed patterns, were in common use by Assyrian and Babylonian architects several hundred years before the Christian era. The brief overview of pottery that follows is, however, generally restricted to the uses of clay for the types of clay objects more commonly regarded as pottery—tableware, decorative objects, the kinds of pieces the user of this book is probably most interested in making. The survey touches only the highest points of a long history, to which countless numbers of craftsmen and artists have contributed millions of pottery pieces in thousands of forms. It will serve only to hint at a few of the myriad patterns of an art that is a vital element in the vast mosaic of human history.

Some historians have suggested that the discovery of fired clay was probably an accident. Perhaps a woven basket lined with clay to make it more useful for holding grain or seeds dropped into a fire. When the basket burned away, the hard and brittle clay form of the basket remained. The theory has plausibility, for it is said that the earliest shards found in all parts of the world share a decorative effect resembling the weave of a basket.

The earliest pottery vessels were shaped entirely by hand, often with techniques still used by studio potters. The potter would take a lump of clay and form a hollow or depression in its center, using the method called pinching; or he would roll the clay into long coils and spiral them into the shape he wished, using the process called coiling.

As the need for a more efficient method of pottery making developed, the early craftsmen devised crude machines that would allow them to work the clay as it turned. Like pottery itself, potter's wheels developed independently in many parts of the world. They were used in Central Asia as early as 3500 B.C. and in Egypt and Crete only a few hundred years later. The first potter's wheels were primitive and awkward; the potters had to squat beside them, turning the table with one hand and working the clay with the other. Later developments, similar to wheels still in use in very primitive areas of the globe, permitted an assistant to turn the wheel with a long pole as the potter worked. The greatest development in pot-

ter's wheels came when someone thought of connecting two platforms by a shaft, one platform to serve as a working surface for the clay, the other platform to be turned by the potter's feet. Thus was invented the kick wheel, fundamentally unchanged to the present day except for refinements in balance and bearings. Such wheels are known to have been in use in Egypt during the reign of the Ptolemys, as early as 150 B.C.

Pottery throws light upon ancient man's social life—his everyday existence; his journeys and migrations; his religious beliefs, superstitions, and rituals; and the evolution of his aesthetic sensitivities. As such, it is not only the object of search by archeologists, but the subject of study by historians with many areas of special interest.

The earliest forms of Egyptian pottery reveal the potter's success in overcoming the natural limitations of his clay to create functional pottery of surpassing beauty. The first pots made from the coarse earthenware clay available in Egypt were red jars, with pointed bottoms to stand in the desert sands; they were undecorated except for the black tops caused when the pots were fired upside down in beds of hot ashes. Liquids placed in such pots seeped through in time, and to provide watertight containers the Egyptians eventually developed the first known glaze, the so-called Egyptian blue glaze, which not only made the pots more functional but opened the way to decorative processes and a wide range of color effects. These were made possible by brushing the unfired glaze with a variety of metallic pigments. The scenes and hieroglyphics decorating Egyptian pottery are invaluable records of the life and cultural values of these ancient people.

Even before the civilization of the Egyptians, however, there existed in the fertile mountain valleys of northern Persia a town life that had reached a high level of development by 5000 B.C. In Persia (now Iran) and the surrounding areas of Iraq and Mesopotamia, pottery making reached a high degree of technical and artistic perfection. Decorated with natural scenes and such animals as the ibex, the eagle, and the bull, the pottery of this region records its people's prayerful respect for the forces of nature.

The development of Greek pottery parallels the rise of Greek commerce. Strictly utilitarian at first, Greek pottery served later to record the rich life and legends at the beginnings of Western civilization. It is highly admired for its pictorial decorations and the mathematical symmetry of its foms. With the rise of the Greek export trade, pottery making became a distinct industry supplying the special needs of the new commerce. Large pots—*amphorae*—were necessary for the transporting of wine and grain; these pots were made in sections on the wheel and then joined when the sections had dried enough to be safely handled. During the many centuries of Grecian civilization, and influenced by the many cultures with which the Greeks traded, pottery decoration underwent numerous changes in decorative styles. The succession of these styles helps to date the pottery and provides clues to the course of Greek commerce. But extending over the whole range of Grecian pottery decoration is an emphasis upon the human form, indicative of the high respect the Greeks had for the human body and human values.

Roman pottery, on the other hand, was generally more practical than Greek pottery, more revealing of a culture concerned with efficiency and production than with the celebration of myth and of the human spirit. The Romans fashioned molds to mass produce such pottery items as lamps, bird cages, and even tickets to gladiatorial exhibitions, and decorated them with scenes revealing contemporary social interests: chariot races, the fights of the gladiators, animal hunts. Though widely distributed because of Rome's military and commercial hegemony throughout Europe and the Near East, Roman pottery never reached the highest aesthetic levels. The wide use of metals such as bronze and silver for tableware seems to have retarded the development of pottery as a major art form, though the pottery known as Arretine ware is remarkable for its delicate designs of natural and human forms.

For several hundred years before the Romans, most of central Italy had been ruled by the Etruscans. Brilliantly artistic, and influenced by the art of Greece and the Near East, the Etruscans left records in many kinds of clay objects, most notably *bucchero* ware, cups and vases made of unpainted black clay, finely shaped and artfully incised.

It was not in the early Western cultures but in the Far East where pottery making reached its zenith as an art form. By the time of China's Sung dynasty (A.D. 960–1279), when ceramic art reached its golden age, the art of working with porcelain was already about two thousand years old. Both the stoneware and the porcelain of this period are characterized by simple and refined forms, their beauty defined by shape, color, and glaze texture. The pottery of the Ming dynasty (1368–1644) is also highly admired,

Fig. 1. Black-figure *amphora,* illustrative of the classical Grecian shape. Athens, about 525 B.C. The depiction of human activities on a central band between geometric patterns at the neck and base was a typical form of decoration. Height: 12 inches. (*Courtesy, M. H. de Young Memorial Museum, San Francisco.*)

particularly the blue and white porcelain and the polychrome wares in brilliant colors made possible by the discovery of overglaze enamel painting.

To some Chinese, porcelain was more precious than gold or silver and was as highly esteemed as jade. The Chinese regarded it with reverence and spoke of it as having "bones" and "flesh," referring to the kaolin (china clay) and the petuntse (china stone) that were its ingredients. The entire field of pottery making was, indeed, more to them than a mere craft. They regarded the making of pottery as a divine act, aided by the gods. One Chinese historian records the tribulations of the divine potter T'ung, who entered his own furnace to aid in the making of a perfect pot. The god's "fat and blood" became the pot's "perfect glaze," his flesh the body

Fig. 2. Chün stoneware from the Honan province during the Sung dynasty or Yüan period (tenth to fourteenth centuries). *Left:* Jardiniere with purple and blue glaze, 6⅜ inches high. *Bottom center:* Purple and blue glaze bulb bowl, 3⅛ inches high and 8⅜ inches in diameter. *Top center:* Gray blue glaze flowerpot, 8¾ inches high. The surface is slightly pitted with "pinholes," the result of the bursting of tiny bubbles in the glaze. *Right:* Blue glaze bowl, 3⅞ inches high and 8⅜ inches in diameter. The insides of the pots are nearly uniformly blue, probably because they were protected from air drafts during firing. (*Courtesy, Asian Art Museum of San Francisco, the Avery Brundage Collection.*)

of the pot, and his "pure spirit" the "blue of the decoration with the brilliant luster of gems."

In both Japan and Korea pottery making was also invested with religious significance in the making of the *chawan,* the ceremonial Raku ware bowls used in the Zen tea ceremony. Usually made by hand though sometimes thrown on a wheel, the deliberately asymmetric bowls were highly valued and often kept in lined boxes of rare wood. Japanese pottery making was profoundly influenced by the Chinese and Koreans and reached its high point long after Chinese pottery had declined and even become imitative of European forms and techniques. It was not until the seventeenth century, when porcelain was

discovered in the Arita district, that the Japanese could rival the Chinese Ming porcelain, which they much admired. Within a few decades, at Arita and Kutani, which became the porcelain centers in Japan for a century, Japanese potters had perfected an overglaze enamel decoration used on the Imari ware and Nabeshima ware they exported to the Western world.

During the long cultural darkness between the classical period and the Renaissance, pottery continued to be made in Europe, but for the most part it was purely functional, with little attention given to the techniques of decoration on the coarse pitchers, bowls, and platters made for domestic use. A notable exception was Spain, where the highly lustrous pieces known as "golden pottery," decorated in arabesque motifs after Moorish influence, were produced.

With the Renaissance came a renewed attention to the arts and crafts, and during the centuries that followed almost every one of the major European countries developed a type of pottery or pottery decoration that has a unique quality and history of its own.

During the fourteenth century, Italy developed the decorative technique of painting tin glaze on earthenware pottery. Known as *majolica,* after the island of Majorca, which had served as a center for shipping similar pottery to Italy from Spain, this pottery was produced in many places in Italy for several centuries. As the making of majolica pottery declined, the technique was taken to other countries, and notably to France, where the tin-glazed earthenware came to be known as *faïence,* after the Italian city of Faenza, where its manufacture had once flourished. In Holland, tin-glazed ware, known as Delft, was first produced early in the sixteenth century.

The most original contribution of France to the craft of pottery came in the sixteenth century through the efforts of a former glass painter, Bernard Palissy. He labored for years, at great personal sacrifice, to develop a technique for tin enameling that would rival the colors of nature. His Palissy ware consisted of dishes to which he affixed in relief casts of small reptiles, fish, and plants, painted in lifelike colors.

It was not until the eighteenth century that Europe was able to produce porcelain like that made in the Far East, though an inferior type of porcelain ware had been made in Italy and France for over two hundred years. The discovery of porcelain in Europe was made by a German alchemist, Johann Friedrich Böttger, during his search for the secret of making gold. He directed the setting up of a factory at Meissen in 1710, and before the end of the century similar factories had been established in France, Italy, Spain, Belgium, Russia, and the Scandinavian countries. The porcelain dishes and figures produced at Meissen, Dresden, Sèvres, and Florence are treasured examples of the highest development of European pottery.

During the eighteenth and nineteenth centuries the experimental potters Josiah Wedgwood and Josiah Spode developed clay bodies and decorating techniques that are used in industrial production to the

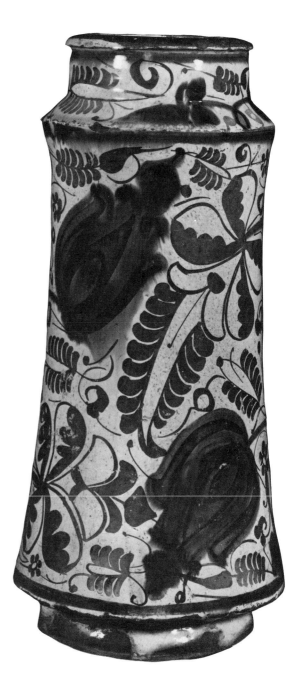

Fig. 3. Spanish *albarrelo* (drug jar), about 1460. Majolica, with luster decoration. Brown and blue floral design on ivory, 12½ inches high, 5½ inches in diameter. (*Courtesy, M. H. de Young Memorial Museum, San Francisco.*)

present day. Wedgwood perfected the production of hard, durable stoneware and earthenware. His most famous stoneware was jasper, a finely grained white body that lent itself beautifully to a wide variety of color stains, particularly the pale blue known as Wedgwood blue. His best-known earthenware was the cream-colored ware still produced as Queen's Ware. Wedgwood's factory in Staffordshire—which he named Etruria in honor of the Etruscan pottery he so greatly admired—produced a wide range of both utilitarian and artistic pottery. Of the latter type, his greatest effort was the reproduction in 1786—after five years of experimenting—of the Portland Vase, a glass vase of great beauty found in Rome during the preceding century and probably made in Alexandria about 50 B.C. Done in jasper with white figures in relief, Wedgwood's vase has been praised as a perfect reproduction of the original.

Spode is credited with the development of bone china, wonderfully strong and translucent, made from kaolin in combination with ground and calcined bones. The commercial success of the tableware he produced early in the nineteenth century was the beginning of the bone china industry still thriving in England today.

Pottery making in the Americas has a history reaching back to the time of the Mound Builders in the Mississippi Valley, the early Indian tribes in the southwestern area of North America, the Mayans in ancient Mexico, and the early cultures in the western mountains and coastal region of South America. Ancient American pottery differs basically from European or Eastern pottery in that the potter's wheel was unknown in America until it was introduced by European colonists. Consequently, much of this ancient pottery was fashioned by the technique of coiling or by the paddle-and-anvil technique, whereby a flat stone or paddle was used to pat a slab of clay into shape around a mold such as a basket. Glazes were almost unknown, and decoration was accomplished by carving or stamping or by applying colored slips, often in geometric designs resembling textile patterns. Pottery produced today by the Indians of the Southwest—in the Hopi and Pueblo villages—is still made and decorated using these traditional, ancient methods.

The primitive pottery of North America was principally functional and was rather unsophisticated in form, but in Central and South America both the decoration and form of the pottery often reflected the complex religions, mythologies, and customs of the cultures. Mayan excavations, for example, have revealed modeled representations of gods and animals; and Peruvian Mochica portrait jars were often given strikingly realistic human forms. Depictions of scenes of daily life on the primitive pottery of America, a great deal of which has survived the ravages of the conquistadors, has told us much of what we know about these ancient civilizations.

Fig. 4. Stirrup spout vessel with hunting scene, showing a deer being driven into nets and killed with spears. North coast of Peru. Height: 12 inches; diameter: 6 inches. Aggressive and warlike, the Moche gave high status to warriors and frequently depicted hunting and battle scenes in clay. Their culture was probably subdued shortly after A.D. 600. (*Courtesy, M. H. de Young Memorial Museum, San Francisco.*)

Since the rise of the industrial age in Europe and America, pottery has been mass produced by craftsmen using techniques that guarantee quantities of identically made tableware, utilitarian objects, and ornamental and decorative pieces. One of these techniques is casting, used in making thin, delicate items, whereby clay in a liquid solution called slip is poured into molds of plaster of Paris. The mold absorbs the water in the clay, leaving a layer of clay on the inside of the mold. When the clay has hardened sufficiently, the excess slip is poured out, the mold is disassembled, and the piece is ready for drying, decorating, and firing.

Another method of quantity production is jiggering, used in making plates and flat pieces. A slab of clay is mechanically pressed over a mold shaped like the top side of the dish. The underside is then shaped by the use of a profile tool that scrapes the clay to the contour of the bottom of the dish.

Even the decorating can be done with mechanical aids. In one method, called decalcomania, the design is applied with engraved plates to tissue paper, which is then placed upon the clay. After the clay has absorbed the colored design, the paper is removed and the pot then fired. This method is also used on glazed ware, which is refired after the application of the design.

Although it can hardly be said that the old, hand methods of making art pottery have ever been completely replaced by mechanical methods, the past few decades have witnessed an accelerating return to popularity of handcrafted pottery along with other arts and crafts. In an age of the mass consumption of mass-produced and depersonalized goods, there is a special attraction in owning and using wares that bear witness to the maker. And in such an age, when most of the things we use are produced for us, there is a further attraction in making some of these items ourselves, in reaffirming the fact that our humanity is at least partially defined by our ability to make and create—to transform raw materials into objects of use and beauty.

CLAY

Although a technical knowledge of clay is not necessary for making a pot, there are certain details that a potter will want to know about the material with which he is working; and there are others—such as what clays to buy for what purposes and at what temperatures different clays can be fired—that are essential for everyday studio activity. The following discussion will treat briefly the origin and nature of clay and the types of clay and their characteristics and uses.

Origin and Nature of Clay

When our world was very young, the earth's surface was composed of a rocky crust formed during billions of years of cooling. As the earth formed an atmosphere, wind and rain and radical changes in seasonal temperatures broke the crust into the particles of rock and soil that now cover the surface of the earth. Just as there are many types of rocks, there are many types of soil, and clay is one of the more common of those types. In its pure form, called *kaolin,* it is the result of the decomposition of feldspathic rock. Chemically, it is a compound of three oxides: one part aluminum oxide (alumina), two parts silicon oxide (silica), and two parts hydrogen oxide (water). The "chemical water" that is removed during the firing process is thus a molecular feature of the clay.

Pure clay, however, is rarely found in nature and is never used by itself as a material for pottery making, its firing temperature being impractically high. However, its whiteness makes it a valuable ingredient in the making of porcelain and china bodies, as well as an ingredient for glazes.

The many types of clay found in nature are the result of different impurities combining with pure clay. When granite decomposed under the effects of decaying organic material and stayed where it decomposed, a clay known as residual or primary clay resulted. But when the clay was pushed by glaciers or picked up by streams and carried to some other place, it came into combination with other minerals and organic matter before it eventually settled in a lake bed or similar hollow area. This clay is known as sedimentary or secondary clay. Such movement broke the particles down to even smaller size, making for greater plasticity. The qualities and characteristics of the different clays available to the potter depend upon the types of impurities that became part of the clay. Pure clay, kaolin, is a primary clay and is usually the principal ingredient in white clay mixtures. Most of the clays used in the potter's workshop, however, are the secondary clays, usually called earthenware and stoneware clays.

All clays share two essential qualities: plasticity and the ability to vitrify. Without the quality of plasticity, clay could be shaped, but it would not hold its shape after being formed. Clay particles are not only extremely small—about seven times smaller in diameter than grains of sand, and vastly thinner—but are flat in shape, so that they stick together whether wet or dry. When they are wet, they slide one upon the other and permit shaping. When they are dry, they adhere to each other and retain their shape. Clay is the only soil with this quality of plasticity. When wet, sand or common topsoil will hold its shape, but when dry it will crumble back into a formless mass.

The second essential quality—the ability to vitrify—is the result of the impurities in clay. These impurities, when subjected to the intense heat of firing, will melt into glass within the clay and bind it in the process called vitrification. Different clays not only have different impurities but also different amounts of impurities and thus vitrify at different temperatures. Stoneware and porcelain are usually fired to the vitrification point, and thereby become watertight. But earthenware clay, which has more impurities, mainly iron, cannot be fired to the vitrification point without melting or losing its shape. As a result, earthenware pots are always naturally porous and will hold water only if they are glazed.

Earthenware, Stoneware, and Porcelain

The three most common types of clay—those available to the potter for general studio use—are earthenware clay, stoneware clay, and porcelain. (For the qualities and characteristics of these three types of clay, refer to the table on page 9.) All are found in nature, but in their natural form the clays do not always have desirable colors, plasticity, porosity ranges, or maturing temperatures. Consequently, most clays used by potters and designated by these terms are, in fact, compounded clays, called clay bodies, specially mixed to achieve specifically desired properties.

Commercially available clays, usually labeled earthenware, stoneware, or porcelain, come dry in fifty-pound bags or wet in plastic-covered packages of various sizes; the twenty-five-pound size is the most convenient for the home potter. The wet clays have been mixed and processed and will need a minimum of preparation. In their plastic containers, they can be stored for long periods without losing their moistness and plasticity. In fact, the longer the clay stays moist, the more it will "age," increasing in plasticity through continued decomposition. Clay packages generally contain information to indicate at what ranges the clay can be fired; the potter then knows whether or not the clay can be fired in the kiln he is using.

Also generally available in suppliers' catalogs are descriptions of the color and texture of the fired clay, glazing suggestions, information on rates of shrinkage and absorption, and recommended uses for the clay.

If you are using a prepared clay body, there are several tests you can perform to determine qualities. As you open the package of clay, sniff it to establish that the clay has a slightly moldy smell. If it does not, store it for a few more weeks, tightly sealed, so that the fine particles of the clay can become perfectly wet. If, on the other hand, the clay passes this test, roll out a small coil and twist it tightly like a pigtail. If it cracks, it lacks plasticity, which is essential for good throwing, and may need further aging. If aging does not correct this problem, the clay body lacks a sufficient amount of plastic clays, and it should be used for sculpture work rather than for throwing. Squeeze some of the clay hard between two fingers. If it contains any grog (bits of fired ground clay), the grog will become visible. Some grog is useful to help reduce shrinkage and to add throwing strength to the clay body.

Unfortunately, you cannot check for color of your clay until you fire it. Even colored catalog pictures showing examples of the fired clay will not show you exactly how the clay will look after it has been fired in your kiln. It is also wise to test each clay you use with your standard glazes, for differences in clay—lightness, darkness, grog, and iron content—will produce differences in the glaze effects.

A newly made piece of pottery will look increasingly small as it dries and is fired. This is because all clays shrink to some extent. Generally, the shrinkage factor is constant for a given clay. In order to calculate the shrinkage factor, follow this simple procedure: Roll out a strip of clay 2 inches wide, a foot long, and ¼ inch thick. Measure the strip in the plastic or raw stage, again after it has dried to the leatherhard stage (firm but still moist), and finally after it has been fired. The changes in the three measurements will indicate the amount of shrinkage to be expected. It is also a good idea, when working with an unfamiliar clay for the first time, to measure the pots when they are moist, again when they have dried in the air, and finally after they have been fired. The amount of shrinkage should be recorded as a guide for making future pots with the same clay. Shrinkage normally runs from 15 to 25 percent, depending upon the composition of the clay body.

The absorption rate will indicate the porosity of the piece when fired at the recommended temperature. Earthenware is never waterproof and has a high absorption rate, sometimes up to 15 percent, which limits its use in making containers to hold liquids, whereas good watertight stoneware and porcelain have an absorption rate of zero.

The following table gives some general information about the three principal types of clay. It should be used cautiously, though, with full awareness that commercially compounded clays are blends that cannot always be neatly classified. The information about firing ranges and the cones at which the clay can be fired will be explained in Chapter 9, "Firing and Kilns." As a rule of thumb, remember that the lower the firing temperature, the more porous and breakable are the finished pots.

Type of Clay	Fired Color	Firing Range for Maturity*	Impurity Content of Ingredients	Characteristics of Finished Pots	Uses
Earthenware	White or cream to red, including tan, brown, and buff.	1830° F. to 2048° F. Cones 06 to 02†	High content of iron impurities, which would bloat or melt at high temperatures.	Soft and porous, rather coarse-grained, easily chipped. Never watertight unless glazed. Porosity range up to 15 percent.	Recommended for pots with medium or heavy walls, made by throwing or hand-building. Must be glazed to hold water.
Stoneware	Light cream to dark buff, including tan, gray, and brown, depending on atmosphere in the kiln.	2232° F. to 2491° F. Cones 6 to 14†	Medium content of calcium, feldspar, and iron. Vitrifies without losing shape.	Hard, dense, finely textured, smooth to coarse (depending on grog content), with high chipping resistance. Porosity from 1 to 6 percent.	Recommended for utility and decorative ware, including dishes, with walls of medium thickness, made by throwing or hand-building.
Porcelain	White to blue white.	2336° F. to 2491° F. Cones 9 to 14†	Blend of kaolin, feldspar, and flint.	Very hard, tough, extremely fine texture; translucent. Acid resistant. Porosity from 0 to 3 percent.	Recommended for delicate pieces with thin walls—dishes and decorative ware. Often used in cast ware, but can be made plastic enough for throwing.

* The temperature at which a clay body fuses and reaches its full development.
† Cones refer to the Orton series. Seger cones have different temperature ranges.

2

Becoming a Potter

THE WORLD OF POTTERY

Pottery making is only one dimension of ceramics. The term "ceramics" comes from the Greek word *keramos,* meaning potter's clay or earthenware, but it has taken on the general meaning of "fired earth" and thus encompasses not only pottery but all fired materials made from earthy substances. Glass making comes within the field of ceramics; and the industrial uses of clay or porcelain include the manufacture of drainage tiles, porcelain sinks, electrical insulators, fine chinaware and earthenware for the table, terra-cotta pots for plants, and the bricks for your home and hearth.

As you become engaged in pottery making, you will find it valuable to visit, if possible, manufacturing plants where fired objects are made. Certainly, you will want to visit local potteries and studios and observe other potters at work. If you live near the large centers of craft activities on the East or West Coast, a weekend outing could be pleasurable and instructive. If you live some distance from such areas, you might wish to plan your vacations with these destinations in mind.

You will want, too, to explore museums and galleries for pottery collections and exhibits, to see the pottery of the past and the present, to get ideas for design and decoration, and to profit from the experience of highly skilled potters. Local newspapers will keep you informed on crafts and art exhibits that you may want to see.

An extremely useful book, first published in 1973 and to be revised periodically, is the *American Crafts Guide* (Gousha Publications, P.O. Box 6227, San Jose, Calif. 95150). Organized by states, the volume is a directory of craft shops, galleries, museums, suppliers, and individual craftsmen throughout the United States. Although ceramics is only one of the many crafts included in the guide, as today's most popular craft it is given extensive attention.

There are several periodicals that contain valuable pottery-making information. *Craft Horizons* includes relevant articles, and *Ceramics Monthly* is devoted exclusively to well-illustrated articles about pottery-making techniques that are helpful to the professional and the hobby potter alike. Subscriptions to these publications are worthwhile investments. *Craft Horizons* is published at 16 East 52nd St., New York, N.Y. 10022, and *Ceramics Monthly* at Box 4548, Columbus, Ohio 43212.

Bookstores and bookshops in museums have crafts sections including books on special phases of pottery making—wheel throwing, hand-building, decoration, glazes, kilns, the history of pottery, and finding and preparing the materials for mixing your own clay and glazes. You will also find that many crafts-supply dealers list books in their catalogs. As your interest and skill in pottery develop, and as you find that you require more specialized information, your local library will probably prove helpful. A useful list of books on clay and pottery-making instruction and history is *Bibliography: Clay,* available from the American Crafts Council, 44 West 53rd St., New York, N.Y. 10019.

There are a few individual titles we advise you to consult. Glenn C. Nelson's *Ceramics: A Potter's Handbook* includes both a well-illustrated discussion of past and contemporary pottery and a detailed survey of studio and commercial pottery making. Daniel Rhodes's *Clay and Glazes for the Potter* and *Kilns: Design, Construction, and Operation* and David Green's *Pottery Glazes* give specialized, authoritative information. Bernard Leach's *A Potter's Book* draws upon a lifetime of dedication to pottery making in both the Far East and England for a discussion of the creative as well as the practical problems of the potter in his studio.

Initially, you will probably keep most of your pottery for your own use. Eventually, however, you will become interested in the work of other potters and will begin collecting pieces you admire. You will also probably begin selling, trading, and giving away pieces of your own. All in all, your pleasure in pottery making will be enhanced immeasurably when you participate in the pottery world fully—as a practicing potter, as an observer and a traveler, and as a reader and collector.

SETTING UP A STUDIO

Working Space

No matter how modest are your beginnings as a potter, you will need a place where you can have your materials and equipment handily together. The larger the space, the better. A complete room or separate building is ideal. But even a small area—a corner in the basement or the garage or the utility room—can be made to serve. Whatever the space, it should have certain equipment and furnishings. It should also be located where some mess and clutter will not bother you. The work area is certain to become dusty and spotted with clay particles and drops of wet clay.

You will need a sturdy table for the basic studio work of wedging, hand-building, applying glazes, and performing the varied processes of making pottery. The surface of the table is not important, save that it be even and level, for an oilcloth spread upside down on it makes a good surface for working clay.

A water supply is strongly advised but not absolutely essential. Even if running water is available, you will need a container (such as a plastic dishpan) next to the sink, partially filled with water so that you can give your hands and tools a preliminary rinsing before washing them in the sink. Avoid getting clay into the sink, for it will quickly clog the pipes. If running water is not available, the plastic container or water bucket by itself will somewhat inconveniently suffice. A paper-towel roller next to your water is another necessity.

Storing and Drying

Above the table or adjacent to it, you should have as many sturdy shelves as you can manage. You will find them necessary for holding your supplies and tools and for drying pots after they have been shaped or glazed. A special storage or drying area, somewhat cool and damp, is ideal, but in its absence you can manage with shelves in your studio and use plastic cloths and bags around your pots to control the rate of drying. Tightly covered pots will dry hardly at all, while loosely covered pots will dry slowly.

If space permits, an old icebox or disconnected refrigerator fitted wth wooden shelves will serve as a good damp box, where unfinished pieces can be stored until you return to them and where newly shaped pieces, called greenware, can be placed for the initial stage of drying. A cabinet may be lined with plastic to serve the same purpose. Even in a damp box, however, clay will turn leatherhard, so stiff that it can no longer easily be shaped. If you plan to return to a piece for further work and wish to keep it moist and pliable, it is necessary to cover it with a piece of plastic or a damp cloth. See Fig. 5 below.

Fig. 5. Properly stored greenware tells the potter at a glance the drying stage of the pots. The pots on the top shelf are completely dry, ready for bisque firing. Those on the center shelf need further drying. Those on the bottom shelf have just either been thrown or trimmed. Placing a pot upside down while drying allows the entire pot to dry at the same rate, helping to prevent the bottom from cracking and warping. Pots with lids should be dried with the lids on. Placing small items on boards makes for ease in handling them. The use of plastic covering keeps pots plastic and slows the rate of drying.

Tools and Equipment

As you work with pottery your stock of tools and equipment will inevitably increase, but certain basic items are essential from the start. Throughout this book there are pictures illustrating the tools and equipment needed for various processes. (See Chapter 3, page 20, for basic wheel-throwing tools; Chapter 6, page 75, for hand-building tools; Chapter 7, pages 84 and 91, for decorating and glazing equipment.) Some of these items you probably already have—sponges, a plastic ruler, a rolling pin, various sizes of cups and containers. Others you will have to acquire. Illustrated on page 14 is a fairly complete selection of supplementary tools for wheel-throwing and hand-building. Beginning potters may not find a need for all of these tools, but the more you have, the easier will be your work with clay. The essential tools are a loop tool, a fettling knife, turning and modeling tools, a potter's knife, a finishing rubber, a cutoff needle, and an elephant ear sponge.

The tools illustrated here are probably available through a local supplier. Thumb through the yellow pages for the names of local studios and dealers. If no local outlets are available, several distributors who regularly advertise in *Ceramics Monthly* will send you catalogs and price lists.

Potter's Wheels and Kilns

The largest and most expensive pieces of equipment you will want are a potter's wheel and a kiln. Potter's wheels are now manufactured throughout the country and are in a variety of types and at a wide range of prices. Both foot-powered kick wheels and motor-driven wheels can be purchased either in kits or as assembled machines, and instructions for making both types are also published for the potter interested in making his own wheel. For the beginner we

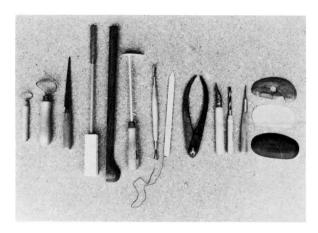

Fig. 6. Tools for making pottery. *Left to right:* (1) handle maker, for pulling through a block of clay to cut a handle; (2) loop tool (or pear peeler), for trimming the base or foot of a pot; (3) fettling knife, for cutting or carving; (4) spongette, for cleaning out water from tall pots; (5) throwing stick, for compressing the bottom and shaping tall pots; (6) turning tool, for trimming the base of a pot while it is still on the wheel; also for leatherhard foot trimming; (7) ribbon or modeling tool, for trimming or carving; (8) mound spear, for trimming and cutting when throwing off the mound; (9) calipers, for measuring lids and pots; (10) hole punch, for cutting round holes in pots such as hanging planters and candleholders; (11) drill, for hole punching, (safer for leatherhard clay than the hole punch); (12) potter's knife, a sharp, double-edged blade for carving hard clay; (13) wooden bowl rib (*top*); flexible steel rib (*center*); finishing rubber (*bottom*)—all of which can be used for shaping the inside and outside of bowls. Each potter seems to have his favorite tool for this purpose. At the bottom center is a piece of nylon cord for cutting clay lumps from the clay block before wedging and pots from the mound or wheel head.

dination between hands and feet that some people find difficult to master. Some kick wheels, however, can be fitted with a motor to ease the drudgery of kicking. The choice of which type of wheel to acquire depends in part on economics and in part on personal preference.

Like potter's wheels, kilns can be constructed from either plans or kits, but the wisest course for the beginner is to purchase either an electric kiln with a firing chamber of about six cubic feet or a gas kiln of the same size that can be fired with either natural gas or propane. Both types sometimes come as modules so that you can reduce or increase the size of the kiln to accommodate the load to be fired. Local dealers can explain the features of available kilns and help you in the selection of the one best suited to your needs. Kilns are discussed further and illustrated in Chapter 9. If you cannot acquire your own kiln, you will probably find that you can hire local potters to do your firing.

The potter's wheel will become a central feature of your studio, but the kiln will very likely be housed elsewhere. Because of both the power source neces-

Fig. 7. Robert Brent potter's wheel, Model C, with a 12-inch aluminum head marked with concentric rings to aid centering. Powered by a ½ horsepower motor, it can center up to 50 pounds of clay and run to a speed of 240 r.p.m. Heel and toe foot pedal, which holds the setting when foot is removed. Operates on standard 110 volt outlet. (*Courtesy, Robert Brent Company, Healdsburg, Calif.*)

recommend a motor-driven, variable-speed wheel. The variable speeds are controlled by a foot treadle. Sturdy, useful wheels of this type can be purchased for around $200, but the more reliable models will very likely cost from $250 to $400. Kick wheels have the advantage of costing much less than electric wheels. Further, some potters prefer them because of their role in the development of pottery and because using them is more suggestive of traditional craftsmanship. Operating a kick wheel hour after hour, however, is very tiring, and it requires a coor-

sary and the heat generated by the kiln, you will probably want to place it in either the garage or the basement—wherever you do not have your studio—or even outside the house. If your studio is sufficiently large, it will be convenient to house the kiln in it—but away from your stored clay and drying pots so that the heat generated by the kiln will not affect them.

WEDGING

The first step in the making of any pottery piece is to wedge the clay. Wedging is the process of kneading clay to make it of even consistency throughout and pounding it to eliminate all pockets of air. This is a necessary step, one that must be done thoroughly, for air left in the clay or an uneven distribution of moisture will cause problems from the initial shaping of the clay through the firing.

As a beginner you will probably find it easier to buy your clay than to prepare it yourself. Clay can be purchased in two forms—separate clays, gen-

Fig. 9. Wedging table for home use, made from a wooden soft drink case filled with plaster. A light wedging table like this one should be anchored so that it will not shift around. When not being used for wedging, it can be used to absorb moisture from overwet clay.

Fig. 8. Robert Brent kick wheel, Model KW. Made of ½-inch exterior plywood. The flywheel uses bricks sandwiched between plywood for weight and ease of balance. Head is 12-inch cast aluminum, with concentric rings. Available assembled or in kits containing metal parts or metal parts and precut plywood. May be converted to electric power. (*Courtesy, Robert Brent Company, Healdsburg, Calif.*)

erally three or more to be mixed yourself, and premixed clay, already moistened and essentially ready for use. If you buy clay mixes, you must dry mix the clays, add sufficient water to make a clay slurry (a thick mixture of water and clay), and then air dry the clay until it is the proper consistency for wedging. (To test for proper consistency, press a thumb into the clay. If clay particles adhere to the thumb, the clay is too wet for wedging.) With this method, the wedging process is extremely important, and you must wedge sufficiently to assure an even consistency and an absence of air pockets.

Buying premixed clay is the easiest and safest course for the beginner. Clay generally comes in twenty-five-pound bags. Before being packaged it will have been mixed thoroughly, pugged (processed through a mill something like a meat grinder to consolidate it), and, by means of a vacuum, relieved of all air. There is therefore very little you must do to prepare it for the wheel. Packaged in plastic containers, commercially prepared clays can be stored for long periods without losing their moistness and plasticity.

Using a nylon clay cutter, cut off a section as large as you will require and round it to a flat top cone ready for the wheel. Since even premixed clays are not always perfectly mixed or de-aired, however, it is wise to check clay carefully before using it. You will need a wedging table or a specially prepared surface. (See Fig. 9.)

Some potters prefer to equip the wedging board or wedging table with a cutting wire (piano wire does fine), stretched taut with a turnbuckle from a board extending up from the back of the table down to the front. They use the wire to cut a lump of clay in half before throwing one-half of the lump down on the table and then throwing the other half down on top of it, repeating the process from six to a dozen times to assure even consistency throughout the clay. With commercially prepared clays, however, the use of a cutting wire is not really necessary; but it is convenient when wedging salvaged clay for reuse.

The following steps are the minimal ones for wedging.

Fig. 10.   Grasp the clay and roll it toward you with both hands.

Fig. 11.   Push down and away with the heels of both hands. Repeat this step several times to assure an even consistency. Take care to avoid folding the clay, thereby allowing air to get trapped inside, or wedging the clay until it becomes dry.

Fig. 12.   Check to see if the clay is thoroughly wedged. Using a nylon clay cutter, cut the clay in half, bend it slightly, and look for air pockets, lumps of dry clay, and soft spots from slip or slurry. After you have checked the clay, pound the two sections together on the table, taking care not to entrap air by hitting the two flat surfaces directly together. Then pound the clay on the table several times to break up any possible air pockets. Finally, roll it into a cone.

Fig. 13. Set the cone upright and pat it into shape, making sure there are no angular edges or flat sides. The rounder you can shape the cone by hand, the less work you need do on the wheel. The clay shown here is roughly conical or mound shaped and is ready for the wheel.

WEDGING PROBLEMS

Fig. 14. Do not permit the clay to flatten out as you roll it or it will extrude beyond your hands and trap air in the folds. This defeats one of the purposes of wedging, the removal of air pockets.

Fig. 15. Avoid folding the clay and thereby trapping air in it. Keep your fingers together as you wedge. Finger holes in the clay will also entrap air.

Fig. 16. This is a section of poorly wedged clay. Bending the clay slightly reveals both large and small air pockets. This clay needs much further wedging, primarily pounding on the wedging table.

RE-USING CLAY

When you make a piece of pottery there is always some leftover clay—excess clay trimmed from the top of a pot, the turnings from trimming the base and walls, and clay that has adhered to the wheel head or bat, to tools, and to hands. An unsuccessful attempt at making a pot need not be a waste of clay. Until clay has been fired, it can be used time and again. It is useful to keep handy a fairly large, covered plastic bucket or crock in which leftover clay can be stored until a sufficient quantity has accumulated for re-use.

When your container is filled with scrap clay, fill it with water and leave it until the clay is thoroughly moistened. Then take out as much as you think you can wedge at one time and set it to air dry on the wedging table, on a concrete slab (such as a driveway or sidewalk, but where it will not be walked on), or on a piece of oilcloth or plastic tarp. Let the clay dry until it is just slightly wetter than it should be for throwing. Divide the clay into equal sections of about five or ten pounds and begin wedging. As you wedge, your hands and the wedging table will continue drying the clay to the proper throwing consistency.

3

Throwing off the Mound: Basic Processes

To a potter the term "throwing" refers to making any form of pottery on a potter's wheel. Whatever the type of wheel, the process is essentially the same: a lump of clay is placed either directly on the wheel head or on a plate or bat affixed to the wheel head and is then centered and shaped into the desired form.

The two principal techniques of throwing are *off the mound* (also called *off the hump*) and *off the head*. To throw off the mound, the potter wedges and centers a mass of clay sufficient for two or three or even four pots, then makes each pot by working with only a portion of the clay at the top of the mound. Throwing off the head involves centering sufficient clay for a single pot. Throwing off the mound is a technique that has long been used by production potters who must make large quantities of identical small pots, but it has advantages over throwing off the head that make it attractive to the beginning potter as well.

First, it is common for beginners working off the head to rub the edges of their hands raw by incorrectly placing them in contact with the wheel head and the coarse, abrasive particles of clay. Throwing off the mound avoids this problem, for the potter's hands are elevated off the wheel.

Fig. 17. Basic tools for throwing. In addition to the potter's wheel (an electric variable-speed wheel is shown here), you will need the following equipment (illustrated clockwise): (1) *cutoff needle,* for trimming rims; (2) *wood knife* or *trimming spear,* for trimming and shaping bottom of pots; (3) *nylon clay cutter,* for cutting pots from the mound or wheel; (4) *elephant ear sponge,* for cleaning the surface of pots while they are on the wheel and for finishing rims; (5) *finishing rubber,* for finishing and cleaning the inside of bowls; (6) *turning tool,* for trimming base of pots. The water bucket contains water and slip (clay in suspension) so that you are not working with pure tap water. The clay, ready for centering, is on a bat, which is used for throwing large forms off the head.

throwing. Since the technique is essentially a process used by production potters, it allows for greater facility in throwing a number of identical or similar objects. Once the potter has learned through experience how much clay to lift and center for a particular type and size of pot, he can repeat the process readily to make matching sets of mugs, goblets, small bottles, and plates.

Throwing off the mound is, in fact, limited to the making of reasonably small pots, such as the beginner is likely to make. Larger pots, which require more clay, must be thrown off the head. Since both techniques are essential skills, they will each be treated in detail. This chapter will deal with the basic processes of throwing, with emphasis upon throwing off the mound and the problems frequently encountered in learning the processes. The next chapter will illustrate making the basic forms of pottery off the mound, and the subsequent chapter will emphasize the technique of throwing off the head and making pots larger than those that can be thrown off the mound.

Second, throwing off the mound encourages the beginner to discard a failure and go on, with minimal new preparation, to throwing another pot. If all the clay that has been wedged and centered is necessary for a single pot, it is natural to continue to putter with it and try to save it simply because it is already on the wheel and the potter is eager to make a pot with it, rather than wedge more clay, center it, and start over. In throwing off the mound, however, he has initially wedged enough clay for several pots; if the first attempt is not successful, he can simply cut the clay off the mound, lift more clay from the mound, and immediately try again.

The third advantage becomes apparent after the beginner has developed the skill necessary for

THE BASIC PROCESSES OF THROWING: MAKING A SMALL CYLINDER

Whichever method of throwing is used, off the mound or off the head, five basic processes are involved. After the clay has been wedged preparatory to making any clay form, it must be placed on the wheel head and forced until it is perfectly in the center. This step is called *centering.* Without perfectly centered clay, the potter cannot create a symmetrical pot with walls of consistent thickness. The next step is *opening,* whereby the potter depresses his thumbs into the revolving clay and then spreads the clay to form walls. Next is *lifting* or *pulling up.* At this time the potter exerts pressure on the walls, lifting them and thinning them simultaneously. After the walls have been lifted, the pot is ready for *shaping* and *finishing.* The final step is *removing* the pot from the mound or from the wheel head.

The instructions that follow demonstrate these five basic processes in the making of a small, cup-shaped pot—a basic cylinder shape—off the mound.

Centering

Fig. 18. Correct body position is essential for successful centering. Lean in well over the clay so that your center of gravity is low and your torso is above the clay. Your arms must be firmly braced—the left elbow locked into the hip so that the forward weight of your body helps to push the left hand against the clay as you pull the clay toward you with the right. Each type of wheel requires a modification of this posture. Basically, though, you must be in a good position to push down on the clay. If your arms are not firmly braced you will discover the clay moving your arms rather than your arms moving the clay.

Fig. 19. Place the rough cone of clay firmly on the wheel head, as well centered as possible within its rings. The bottom of the cone should be somewhat rounded so that when it is placed on the wheel head it will not trap any air and will firmly adhere to the wheel head. Pat the cone down firmly on the sides to anchor the clay. As the wheel turns slowly, and with your hands dry, pat the clay into as even a cone as possible. Then, with your hands and the clay both wet, and with the wheel at high speed, lean well over the wheel so that you are looking almost directly down at the clay. Let your hands ride freely on the clay to build up slip. As your hands dry, wet them again, using a minimum amount of water. Do not add so much water that the clay becomes sloppy.

Fig. 20. With your left elbow locked firmly against your hip, push at the base of the clay with the heel of your left hand, at the same time pulling the clay toward you with your right hand. Fingers of both hands should be held tightly together.

Fig. 21. Follow the clay upward as your hands continue to force it toward the center of the wheel—the left hand pushing away from you, the right hand pulling toward you. Take care to keep your hands moving upward with the clay so it is not cut off by them.

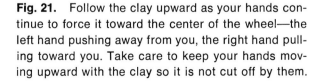

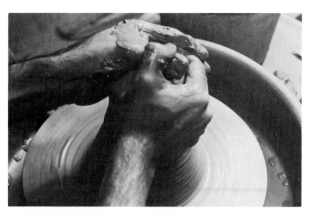

Fig. 22.   When your hands reach the top, place your left hand immediately atop the cone and then start pushing down. Now your right arm should be braced so that your right hand is very firm. (Reverse hand positions if you find that you work more comfortably with your left arm braced and your right arm used for pushing down.)

Fig. 23.   With your left hand atop the cone, your right arm still firmly braced, your right hand on the side of the cone, and the fingertips of both hands slightly overlapping, push the clay down slowly and carefully with the left hand and with the right hand hold the clay in control. Pushing down on the clay not only removes any remaining air bubbles, but reduces the clay to a flat-topped mound. Repeat the upward and downward movements (as in Figs. 21 and 22) until you have a reasonably well-centered mound of clay (see Fig. 24).

Fig. 24.   Grasp the cone at the top. This is the portion you will center. Make a slight indentation with your little finger to identify that portion. (Before you try to center with both hands together, go through the motions with each hand separately to see what they will be doing.) The right hand pinches the clay, pulls it toward you, and lifts it up slightly.

Fig. 25.   The left hand folds over the top and side of the clay and pushes down and into the right hand.

Fig. 26. You are now working with only the top portion of the clay. Again use your hands as opposing forces, pinching the clay with your right hand and pulling toward you and up. The left hand will overlap the right, the fingers pulling against the right hand, the palm and heel pushing down and into the right hand. The arms must be well braced. When the two opposing pressures become equal, the clay will center. When you think it is centered, release your hands cautiously; a sudden, jerky motion can move it off center. Check the centering by holding a steady finger alongside the clay as it revolves. The finger should ride evenly on the surface.

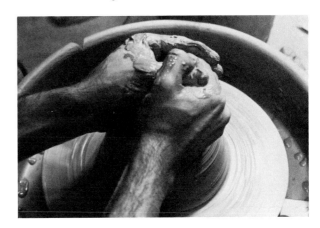

Centering Problems

Fig. 27. This cone is both poorly shaped and exaggeratedly placed off center on the head. It should be worked more on the wedging table to remove the corners and molded into a conical shape. It should also be placed as close to the center of the wheel head as possible, using the scored circles of the head as guides. For correct clay formation, see Fig. 19.

Fig. 28. If your hands are open and cupped rather than fully on the surface of the clay as you move them upward, the edges of the hands will cut into the clay and separate it. The hands must be completely on the clay, covering a broad area. This error can be corrected by using both hands while the wheel turns to push the clay down into a fairly conical shape again. Refer to Fig. 21.

Fig. 29. If your hands are not together as you push downward, or if you permit your fingertips to move into the clay rather than work along the surface, a mushroom shape will result. The hands should be joined together, the thumbs and the fingertips of both hands overlapping. This clay must be reshaped by following the centering steps described with Figs. 21 and 22. Failure to hold the clay with one hand as you push with the other causes severe undercutting and flattening.

Fig. 30. The hands here are not only improperly apart, but the heel of the left hand is exerting pressure at the center of the clay rather than on its outside. The result is a depression or cup-shaped hole. The best way to correct this problem is to remove the clay entirely, wedge it again, and start over. Refer to Fig. 22.

Fig. 31. The purpose of centering is not only to get the clay positioned properly on the wheel head, but to achieve a shape that will permit you to move on to opening. This centered clay is too wide and flat, a result of the potter's failure to hold the clay in with one hand as the other pushed down (see Fig. 23). A shape such as this would be proper for a plate or a very wide bowl, but it is too wide to permit separating a section for throwing off the mound or making the proper opening for a small pot. To correct this error, follow the directions in Fig. 19.

Fig. 32. Unless the top of the clay is relatively flat, there is no room for the thumbs to open the clay. This problem was caused by failure to apply pressure on the top of the clay. To correct this problem, follow the directions in Fig. 23.

Opening

Fig. 33. Once centered, the clay must be opened. Again brace your arms, place both hands on the clay, the left fingers overlapping the right, with the thumbs at the top center. Start pushing the thumbs into the center of the clay slowly and evenly as the wheel turns at moderate speed.

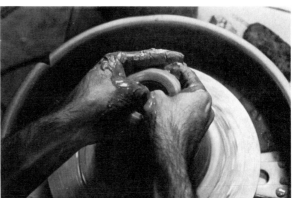

Fig. 34. Without changing the position of your hands, push the thumbs as far down as they will naturally go. (By keeping your hands in position, you will not depress your thumbs below the level that will form the base of the pot.) Then press the thumb tips toward the palms of the hands to open the bottom slightly wider than the top.

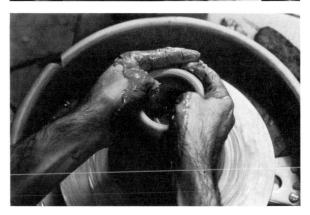

Fig. 35. Keeping the fingers overlapped, change the positions of the thumbs so that you are pressing with the entire side of each thumb against the clay.

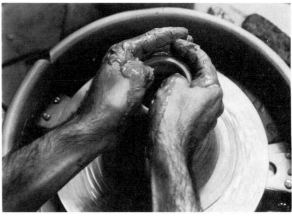

Fig. 36. While pressing the clay between the thumbs and the palms, start to *collar* the clay—that is, push in toward the center with both hands, lifting the hands and smoothing the clay upward so that the outside walls become relatively smooth.

Fig. 37. At this point the cylinder atop the mound should be shallow, stubby, and slightly concave. You are now ready to begin lifting or pulling up the cylinder.

Opening Problems

Fig. 38. Attempting to open the clay before it is perfectly centered results in an off-center opening, the wall thicker on one side than the other. Continuing from this point will only create more problems as the walls are lifted and become thinner.

Fig. 39. The opening has been made too wide for pulling up a cylinder; the walls have been pinched too thin by the thumbs. The hands must be kept together to keep the cylinder narrow.

Lifting

Up to this point you have been working directly over the clay. For the purpose of lifting, however, you must change your body position so that you are able to see the right side of the clay.

Fig. 40.   Lean to the right so that your head and torso are over your right side. (This body position is illustrated in Chapter 5, Fig. 100.) With your right elbow locked into your right hip, your right arm firmly braced, and your left hand inside the clay, lift the clay with the tightly held fingers of the right hand, using the fingers of the left hand to back up the pressure of the right hand. (Some potters prefer to lift with the knuckles of the right hand.) Both hands should be kept together, the thumbs touching or locking, the left hand slightly above the right. In lifting the clay, rock the torso back slightly, using the waist motion to help in the lifting. Keep hands together. Lift slowly and deliberately, maintaining a moderate to fast wheel speed. Too rapid an upward motion will result in an uneven thickness in the walls and a corkscrew effect. The rate of the upward movement should cause the finger ridges to be from ⅛ to ¼ inch apart.

Fig. 41.   Relax the pressure as you reach the top and release pressure completely as your hands come off the clay at the rim.

Fig. 42.   The thickness at the base will be greater than that of the walls. Beginning at the bottom, repeat the lifting process to thin out the walls of the cylinder. The ridge on the outside is caused by the position of the left hand above the right. This position helps prevent the top from flaring out excessively during the raising of the cylinder.

Fig. 43. It is likely that at the end of the lifting process the top edge will be uneven and will need trimming prior to finishing. If so, cut off about ⅜ inch at the top, or however much is necessary, with a cutoff needle. Hold the needle with both hands, keeping one or two fingers of the left hand inside the wall to keep the trim from collapsing because of the pressure of the needle. Push the needle through slowly, with the wheel at moderate speed.

Fig. 44. Use controlled pressure of the fingertips to finish off the top edge. Movements of the hands and fingers should be very slow and deliberate, for the walls are thin and any rapid movement could destroy the pot.

Lifting Problems

Fig. 45. Pulling up too much clay results in a thick top edge. This edge must be thinned out, then the rest of the clay pulled up to thin out the walls of the cylinder gradually.

Fig. 46. The clay has been pulled too thin and is twisted as a result. The uneven top resulted from an uneven pressure between the hands as the cylinder walls were lifted. Hands must be kept rigidly together to maintain even and equally opposite pressure.

Fig. 47. This illustration shows an uneven wall thickness caused by uneven pressure of the hands as the walls were pulled up. The hands must be kept together as shown in the earlier illustrations.

Shaping and Finishing

Fig. 48.   The process of shaping—in this instance the shaping of a cup or mug—is begun inside at the base. Apply a slight pressure with the left hand, using the right hand to control the shape from the outside. Bring both hands up the side walls to shape the pot. Too much pressure from the left hand will collapse the pot.

Fig. 49.   Compress the top with a slight pressure downward from the right forefinger, controlling the clay with the fingers of the left hand. This compression helps eliminate rim cracks and is vital on larger pots.

Fig. 50.   A final finish is given with a moistened elephant ear sponge. Round off the rim and clean up the surface of the pot as well. Remove excess moisture from the inside of the pot. On the finished cup (see Fig. 52), the decorative ridge has been applied with the right thumbnail.

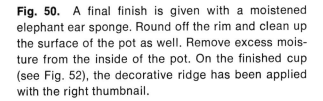

Shaping Problems

Fig. 51. Walls will sag or slump if they are shaped out too rapidly or too close to the horizontal. They must have a gradual slope and not be shaped hurriedly.

Removing

Fig. 52. Use a wood knife or mound tool to trim and shape along the bottom side of the pot before cutting it off. Hold the tool steadily with both hands and move it down and under the pot slowly as the wheel turns at moderate speed, thereby creating a flat surface on the mound so that the pot can be cut off evenly. Push the tool toward the center, but not all the way through.

Fig. 53. Loop a nylon clay cutter around the base with the ends toward you. Holding the ends close to the pot, turn the wheel slowly and pull the string toward you. Keep the string parallel to the wheel head as you pull.

Fig. 54. Scissor the pot at the base as far as you can reach, twisting the pot slightly to release it from the mound, and lift it off. You may also turn the wheel slightly afterward; the wheel motion will release the pot so that you can remove it.

At this point you are ready to lift up and center another portion of the clay to make another pot.

Finishing and Removing Problems

Fig. 55. The two pots illustrate the differences between good work and poor work. The pot on the left has been finished and removed properly. The pot on the right was not finished (usually done with an elephant ear sponge), was not trimmed at the base to indicate a cutoff line, and was cut off unevenly.

LOOKING AHEAD

You have gone through the multiple process of making a single pot off the mound and have probably developed a respect for clay that you lacked before. Watching an experienced potter smoothly, even rhythmically, transform a lump of clay into a symmetrical shape suggests that the clay almost grows by itself, so organic does the process appear. For the beginning student at the wheel, the first attempt at throwing—and even the second, third, and fourth —can be discouraging, but it is well to remember that throwing is an art learned only through repetition and by profiting from one's mistakes. It is a complicated art, calling for muscular strength and coordination, manual dexterity, a sense of form and proportion, a familiarity with the feel of clay, and

persistence—the last in large amounts. As with any other skill, however, practice makes perfect: if you keep at it you, too, will become an experienced potter who can transform clay from a lump into a beautiful piece of pottery.

The end of the throwing process, or of any construction process, leaves the pot far from completed. It must still be stored and dried to await trimming, then bisque fired. It will normally be decorated and glazed and fired again. These processes and techniques are discussed in the following chapters: Chapter 2—storing and drying; Chapter 5—trimming; Chapter 7—decorating and glazing; Chapter 9—firing.

SUMMARY

Throwing a Cup off the Mound: Basic Steps

Centering

1. Place the clay as close to the center of the head as possible. Pat it firmly to make a cone shape and to anchor it to the head.
2. Lean in *over* the clay, tight to it and to the wheel. Lock left elbow into hip or side. Brace both arms firmly.
3. With wheel at fast speed, move clay by pushing with heel of left hand, pulling toward you with the right. Follow the clay up with both hands to form a cone.
4. Push down with one hand. Control side with the other.
5. Repeat step 3 to bring up a low mound. You may need to repeat steps 3 and 4 several times to achieve the low mound.
6. Center top portion. Hands are in opposition—the right pulling, pinching, and lifting, the left pushing down and into the right hand.

Opening

1. Place both hands on the centered mound, left over right, with fingers definitely overlapped.
2. With wheel at moderately fast speed, push in with thumbs as far as they will go.
3. Open across with thumb tips at base of opening.
4. Pinch clay between thumb and palm of both hands. Collar in with both hands at the same time.

Lifting

1. Lean to the right side, with right elbow locked into hip.
2. Set the left hand inside pot, the right hand outside at base of opening. Lock thumbs together. Tighten fingers to form rigid unit.
3. With wheel at moderate speed, lift the clay, using right hand pressure backed up by the left.
4. Use heavier pressure at base, easing off at rim.
5. Repeat lifting until walls are thinned.

Shaping and Finishing

1. With wheel at moderate speed, push across slowly at inside base with left hand.
2. Slowly bring up left hand inside to shape the pot, using right hand outside to control shaping.
3. Finish rim and outside with fingers and elephant ear sponge.

Removing

1. Hold the mound spear or wood knife firmly with both hands.
2. With wheel at moderately fast speed, cut in under the pot, following its downward curve.
3. Loop twisted nylon cutoff around base. Turn wheel *very slowly* and pull string through with right hand. Keep string parallel to wheel head.
4. Scissor the pot with fingers, lift it off, and set it aside.

4

Throwing off the Mound: Basic Forms

After you have learned the process of centering and feel reasonably comfortable in slapping a mass of clay on a wheel head and molding small cylindrical pots, you are ready to extend your skills to other basic forms, that is, to other forms of the cylinder and to the bowl. Variations of these forms result in a variety of pots. The cylinder, for instance, is the basic form not only for cups but for pitchers, vases, bottles, jars, canisters, and goblets; and the bowl shape, or open form, is the basis for bowls of all shapes as well as for casseroles, planters, ashtrays, and plates. Most shapes can be thrown off the mound, but the larger pots, which require a considerable amount of clay, will be discussed in the following chapter, which deals with throwing directly off the wheel head.

THE BOTTLE

The bottle is a variation of the cylinder discussed in Chapter 3. In making a bottle the beginning steps will be those already illustrated under centering, opening, and lifting up, except that at the end of the lifting process the top edge of the bottle should be somewhat thicker than a cup's, so that the clay at the neck will not ripple or fold during collaring.

Fig. 56. At the beginning of the shaping process, the top edge of bottle should be somewhat thick. Compare this illustration with Fig. 49 in the preceding chapter to note the difference between the cup and the bottle.

Fig. 57.   Using the shaping techniques discussed in the preceding chapter, work the bottom and side walls until they are as thin as you wish. Shape the outside wall only as much as you did for a cup. Too much shaping will collapse the bottle. Clean out excess water with a sponge. Use the entire surface of both hands to collar in. Work over a broad area of the pot, not just at one point, always starting low and lifting the hands upward as you collar in. Lift both hands simultaneously so that they are always opposite each other.

Fig. 58.   Collaring will make the clay thicker. To thin it without making it wider, pinch the clay with the fingers of the left hand and push straight in and up under the left thumb with the fingers of the right hand. Work slowly and carefully.

Fig. 59.   Continue to lift upward with the right hand, pushing gently toward the center of the wheel. Avoid making rim too thin and wet, either of which will cause the edge to ripple as you collar in. (See Fig. 64.)

Fig. 60. Repeat the collaring process until you have achieved the desired neck shape (see Fig. 66 for common problem). If there is water in the bottom, use a spongette to remove it.

Fig. 61. To complete the thinning and shaping of a bottle rim is indeed a delicate operation and requires the utmost control and coordination. Pressure should be exceedingly light, the rim turned out very slowly while the wheel is at moderate speed.

Fig. 62. Finish the rim with an easy touch of the fingertips. Clean the rim with a sponge. At this point many potters blow briskly into the bottle. The blowing serves two purposes: it rounds out and softens the shape and it provides a test for the thickness of the walls. If they are too thick, the "poofing" will have no effect. If they are too thin, they will collapse.

Fig. 63. Use a wood knife or mound tool at the base of the curve to cut down and under the bottle and make a flat surface on the mound (see Figs. 52 to 54 in the preceding chapter). Use a nylon clay cutter to cut through the clay, and remove the bottle.

BOTTLE PROBLEMS

Fig. 64. If the edge is too thin, it will ripple. Use a needle to cut off the rippled clay (see Fig. 65) and collar in again. If the edge still ripples, very likely the walls are too thin. Begin on another pot, remembering to leave the rim and the walls a little thicker.

Fig. 65. To trim off an uneven or thin rim, grasp a needle in the right hand, directing it with the forefinger. Brace your arm securely to assure a straight cut. Support the inside wall with the fingers of the left hand so the wall will not collapse. Depending on the thickness of the wall, allow from three to five revolutions of the wheel while you cut through. Wheel should be turning moderately fast. Cut off only what you must, just below the problem area. Lift off and discard the clay peel.

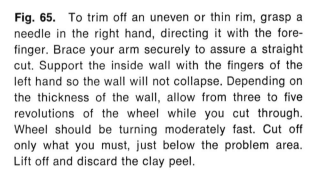

Fig. 66. This bottle has been pushed in too sharply at one point and will probably collapse. There is also the likelihood that the severe constriction will cause the neck to rip off. This problem can be avoided by lifting during the collaring.

JAR AND LID

The jar shape differs only slightly from the cup shape (see Fig. 52 in the preceding chapter). The rim of the jar must be more pronounced and flared slightly more than on the cup in order to accommodate a lid. Except for this one difference, however, the shaping process for the jar is the same as for a cylinder or cup (see Chapter 3, Figs. 48 to 50).

Fig. 67. Use calipers to measure the inside of the rim. Leave calipers open at this width and set aside for use in determining the size of the lid.

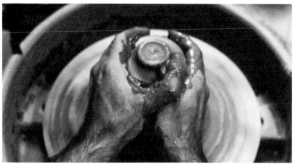

Fig. 68. To make the lid, center a small amount of clay. Open the clay about 1 inch from the center, leaving a knob of clay for the lid handle.

Fig. 69. Hold hands steady and together and open the lid handle with index finger. Take care not to make the opening in the lid deeper than its flange.

Fig. 70. Shape the flange of the lid by pinching the clay between the index fingers of both hands. Proceed slowly, for excessive pressure will thin out the flange too much, causing a collapse or loss of shape.

Fig. 71. Use finger to narrow the neck of the handle. With calipers, determine the size of the lid, which must be exactly the width of the inside of the rim. If the flange is too wide, trim with a needle. If too small, flatten to the proper size. Trim base with wood knife as in Fig. 63. Remove the lid from the mound.

GOBLET (CUP AND STEM)

A goblet is made by joining the cup with a stem that requires the centering of approximately the same amount of clay. The difference between making the cup and the stem begins at the opening process (see Fig. 33 in the preceding chapter), for the stem opening is narrower than the cup's and is done with one thumb rather than both. The cup and stem are joined when they have dried to the leather-hard stage. Since the thin rim of the stem will normally dry faster than the cup, it will be necessary to take precautions, such as wrapping the stem in plastic or in a damp cloth, to slow its drying rate. To join the cup and stem, crosshatch the bottom of the cup and the top of the stem with a needle, wet both surfaces with slip, and join them together, taking care that the cup sits perfectly straight on the stem and is perfectly centered. (See Fig. 88 for an illustration of scored surfaces.) In the following illustrations you will note that the stem is always thrown upside down.

Fig. 72. After centering about the same amount of clay required for a cup, open as for a cup, with the left fingers overlapping the right, but using only one thumb for the opening. Keep the diameter of the clay narrower than for the cup during both the opening and the lifting.

Fig. 73. Using both hands, lift the clay and force it toward the center. The right thumb will be pinching the clay against the palm of the hand, the left hand holding the clay in.

Fig. 74. Conclude the first lifting by shaping the top (the foot of the stem) to the desired width. This should be approximately the same diameter as the neck of the goblet cup, that is, slightly smaller than its widest section. Finish the edge of the rim at this point.

Fig. 75. Collar the stem slowly, using the hands to cover a broad area and thereby control the wobbling of the wide top. Carry the hands to the outer edge of the rim, avoiding pressure that would change the width of the top.

Fig. 76. Using a wood knife, score the clay at the point where it is to be cut through with a nylon cutter. The surface where the cut is made must be absolutely flat so that the cup will not tilt when it is joined to the stem.

Fig. 77. Gently grasp the stem and lift it off with the aid of a wood knife. Let it dry upside down.

THE BOWL

The centrifugal force that tends to throw the clay outward as it revolves on the wheel accounts for the primary difference between cylinder throwing and bowl throwing. In making a cylinder, the left hand is often employed to hold the clay in as the right hand shapes it. But in bowl throwing, the clay is permitted to some degree to follow its own natural tendency to flare outward from the center of the wheel. The potter, therefore, is working *with* the clay, gently aiding or inhibiting its natural outward movement, whereas he is essentially working *against* the clay when he throws a cylinder. This is not to say that bowl making is easier than cylinder making, for each basic form has its particular difficulty—the

cylinder in the lifting process and the bowl in the control necessary for shaping its walls as they flare outward.

Bowl throwing involves exactly the same procedures as the cylinder in the centering and opening processes. The difference begins with lifting. In lifting a cylinder, the left hand is above the right hand; in making a bowl, the fingers are opposite each other. To begin the bowl, follow the basic processes in the preceding chapter through Fig. 37. Then turn to the following sequence of illustrations, noting that whereas in lifting the cylinder the movement was straight upward, now it is both upward and outward.

Fig. 78. Place fingers of each hand opposite one another. With the wheel at slow to moderate speed, move hands slowly, controlling the outward shaping and pulling with the right hand.

Fig. 79. With the right hand, push the rim inward to control shaping. Pinch clay between the fingers to thin it to the desired thickness.

Fig. 80. As you determine the shape of the bowl you wish to make, fix the right hand firmly in the shape you wish. With the left hand inside the bowl, exert pressure against the template or mold formed by the right hand.

Fig. 81. Compress the rim to prevent cracking later. Pinch rim with the left hand as you push down with the right forefinger.

Fig. 82. Use a finishing rubber or bowl rib to smooth the inside of the bowl and complete the shaping. Smooth the edges of the rim with a sponge or strip of chamois. Trim and remove bowl from mound.

BOWL PROBLEMS

Fig. 83. Opening too quickly or letting your hands separate during the opening will reduce control of the clay.

Fig. 84. Trimming too shallowly at the base will create two problems. First, you are likely to cut a hole in the bottom, particularly if the inside base was not flat. Second, since the shallow trimming has reduced the strength of the base, the pot may collapse as it is lifted off.

Fig. 85. A variety of pots can be thrown off the mound. Heights range from the small weed pots and cups of slightly over 2 inches to the goblet, which is nearly 8 inches. The decorations illustrate the minimal designs appropriate for small pieces of pottery. (*Two goblets by Jay Trenchard; mug by Steve O'Loughlin; candle holder on wooden block by Judy Pitkin.*)

THE TEAPOT

The three basic pieces that make up a teapot can be thrown off the mound using three portions of one centered mass of clay. Since the spout and lid are smaller than the body of the teapot, they are thrown first, leaving the remaining clay for the body. Even if all three pieces are thrown on the wheel head, it is best to make the lid before the body, for the neck of the pot can be collared in to fit the size of the lid more easily than the latter made to fit the former. The lid is thrown upside down, with a fairly long stem that will reach down inside the pot and keep the lid from falling out during pouring (see Chapter 5, Fig. 125, showing a casserole lid). Making the spout requires essentially the same techniques as in making a small bottle. The neck opening should be at least ½ to ¾ inch wide to permit easy pouring.

Fig. 86. To join the spout, set it against the side of the teapot, and score a line around the base of the spout to indicate where it will attach. Make certain the pouring tip of the spout is *above* the water line of the teapot.

Fig. 87. Cut out the holes for the water. They must be large enough (approximately ⅜ inch) not to fill up with glaze during the firing. Six or eight holes are sufficient.

Fig. 88. Using crosshatch scoring, vigorously score the base of the spout and the corresponding area on the teapot. Wet the scored area of the spout and add slip to the teapot. Slip is absolutely necessary, for there is no way to join the spout from the inside. The slip will fill in and seal the joint. Press on the spout, and press in the edges. Smooth over the seam.

Fig. 89. Handle lugs (for bamboo handles) can be made either by pulling or from coils of clay. Score and attach them. If bamboo handles are not available, a pulled handle can be attached at the back, exactly opposite the spout. Note that the long stem on the lid prevents the lid from falling out when the pot is tipped for pouring.

Fig. 90. Teapot and tea bowls done wholly on the mound. The tea bowls were thrown off the top of the mound, followed by the spout and lid, and finally the pot itself with the remaining clay.

SUMMARY

Basic Forms off the Mound

Bottle

1. Lift cylinder as for a cup, leaving a slightly heavier rim.
2. Shape as for a cup.
3. Collar in with both hands, lifting slightly.
4. Thin out neck by pushing clay with fingers of left hand and pushing in and up under left thumb with fingers of right hand.
5. Continue collaring to desired size by pushing gently toward center of wheel.
6. Finish rim with fingertips.
7. Trim and remove as for a cup.

Lid

1. Center a flat mound.
2. Open about one inch off center, leaving knob.
3. Open knob with index finger.
4. Pull out flange between right and left forefingers.
5. Trim and remove.

Goblet Stem

1. Center very narrowly.
2. Open with one thumb and collar in narrowly.
3. On the first lift with both hands, shape the rim edge (foot) to desired size.
4. Using hands to cover a broad area, collar in stem to desired size.
5. Score, cut off, and remove.

Bowl

1. Center and open as for a cylinder, but pull wide.
2. Turn wheel at slow to moderate speed. Pinch clay between fingers of both hands.
3. Pinch and lift, controlling shape with right hand.
4. Compress rim with right forefinger while controlling rim between left forefinger and thumb.
5. Shape with rib from inside.
6. Smooth edges with sponge.
7. Trim and remove.

5

Throwing off the Head: Basic Processes and Forms

The beginning potter who has become familiar with the basic processes of throwing by working off the mound can move with relative ease to throwing directly off the wheel head. Indeed, to some extent he is already working directly on the head when he takes a large mass of clay and roughly centers it on the head prior to separating a small mass for fine centering at the top of the mound. Throwing off the head requires the perfect centering of the large mass of clay and the use of all the clay for a single pot. Both techniques involve the same processes, but the larger mass, because of its size and weight, is more difficult to control and shape. For this reason, the wheel speed during centering, as well as during all other basic processes, should be slower than for throwing off the mound.

When throwing off the mound the beginner should try to center the large mass almost perfectly. In this way, he will have a headstart when he begins throwing off the head. It should be recognized, too, that any pot thrown off the mound can also be thrown off the head. The reasons for throwing off the mound are to reduce the time spent in the preparatory processes of wedging and centering and to encourage the beginner to discard a failure and move on without having to face the somewhat dreary chore of further wedging.

USING A BAT

In throwing a large pot it is necessary to work on a bat, a round slab attached to the wheel head that permits the potter to remove the pot from the head without distorting it through handling. The bat also serves as a tray for carrying and drying. It is an extension of the wheel head and must be firmly attached to it. Some wheel heads are equipped with round pins onto which a bat, with corresponding holes, can be placed. On these constructions, the bat is automatically centered and rests snugly of its own weight on the wheel head.

Bats are available from suppliers in particle board, aluminum, and plaster. Plaster bats and particle board bats are also easily constructed. Since plaster breaks easily, however, there is some advantage to using particle board. To make a particle board bat, use a jig saw or coping saw to cut a round piece of ½-inch to ¾-inch board about 10 or 12 inches in diameter. The material is readily available where lumber supplies are sold. If your wheel head has pins, drill holes in the bat to match the pins. If it does not have pins, do the following:

Fig. 91. Spread soft clay evenly on the wheel head as the wheel turns. (*Caution:* if the clay is unevenly thick at the center, the bat will rock and come off.)

Fig. 92. Roughen the surface of the clay by drawing the fingers through it.

Fig. 93. Dampen the bottom of the bat and press it down hard on the wheel head. New bats may not stick well until they have been broken in, but it will help to roughen the bottom of the bat by scratching it with a sharp tool. Before placing the clay on the bat, dampen the surface of the bat. Do not use too much water, however, or the clay will not stick.

Plaster bats may be made by using 10-inch pie tins, with smooth bottoms, as molds. To mix the plaster, add the necessary amount of water to a bucket, using one pie tin of water for each bat you plan to make. Following the directions on the package, sprinkle the required amount of plaster evenly onto the entire surface of the water and allow it to settle for about five minutes. Then mix the plaster and water thoroughly with one hand, keeping the hand immersed in the water to prevent adding air bubbles to the mixture. Take care to break up all lumps. When the plaster is ready, brush the inside of the pie tins with tincture of green soap, which acts as a separator between the metal and the plaster. Pour the plaster into the pie tins. Work quickly, for casting plaster sets about ten minutes after it has been mixed.

To attach a plaster bat, take some clay slip from the water bucket and spread a thin layer on the bottom of the bat. Push the bat down hard on the dry, clean wheel head. Let the slip harden to hold the bat. Plaster bats must also be moistened considerably on top to hold the clay. When dry, the plaster will in turn dry out the bottom of the clay, releasing it from the bat.

THE CYLINDER: BASIC PROCESSES (VASE)

Centering

The beginning steps for centering on the head are the same as for throwing off the mound. You should be leaning well over the clay, your arms firmly braced to permit maximum control of your hands. The left hand pushes at the base of the clay; the right hand pulls. After the clay has been forced to the center of the wheel and up into a high cone, proceed as follows:

Fig. 94. Gradually push down and let the clay spread out slowly.

Fig. 95. When the clay is flat, return hands to the original position, with the left elbow tucked in, the heel of the left hand pushing, the right hand pulling. The fingers of both hands should point down slightly, the thumbs over the top of the clay. The hands will thus completely contain the clay. Vary the pressure between the hands until the clay begins to center. Check for perfect centering by holding a finger on the surface of the clay as it turns.

Opening

Fig. 96. Keeping the arms well braced, begin opening with the thumbs. The hands ride the mound of clay with a slight pressure inward. The thumbs will not reach down far enough to open the bottom of the large mass of clay.

Fig. 97. Complete the opening with the fingers of the left hand. Lock thumbs together to maximize control. Use needle occasionally to check the depth of the opening. The base should be about ⅜ inch thick.

Fig. 98. With hands in same position, begin pulling straight across with the left hand, the right hand exerting opposite pressure on the outside. (Reverse hand positions if you are more comfortable pulling with the right hand.) Pull slowly; the pull rings inside will be about ⅛ inch or less apart if you are pulling at the proper speed.

Fig. 99. When the clay is properly opened it will be barrel-shaped on the outside. Collar in slightly to straighten the sides.

Lifting and Shaping

Fig. 100. Change your body position to begin lifting the walls. The right arm should be firmly locked into the hip, the left arm tight against the side. With fingers together and hands opposite each other, exert firm pressure with the right hand.

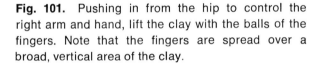

Fig. 101. Pushing in from the hip to control the right arm and hand, lift the clay with the balls of the fingers. Note that the fingers are spread over a broad, vertical area of the clay.

Fig. 102. As the cylinder rises during the second pull upward, the hands will naturally move apart, though the fingertips will be almost opposite each other, with the fingertips of the left hand (inside the cylinder) slightly above those of the right hand (outside the cylinder). Keep the fingers firmly locked together to prevent wobbling. Holding a sponge in the right hand may help you keep your hands from drying out over the long pull on the cylinder.

Fig. 103. Begin shaping the pot after the walls are the proper thickness (¼ to ⅜ inch, depending on the size of the pot). The shaping is begun at the base, with the left hand exerting a slight outward pressure, while the right hand contains and directs the shaping.

Fig. 104. Trim the base with either a wood knife or turning tool. Then complete the shaping by using both hands to collar in the top part. Squeeze in gently with an even pressure and avoid an abrupt change in the line of the curve.

Fig. 105. The finished vase. The rim and surface are finished with an elephant ear sponge, then smoothed with slight pressure from the fingertips before the pot is released from the bat.

Removing

Fig. 106. Use a nylon cutoff to release the pot from the bat. While the wheel turns at moderate speed, keep the string taut and pull it evenly under the pot. Take care to keep it snugly on the bat so that it will not ride up and cut into the base. After the pot is released from the bat, release the bat and take it, with the vase still on it, to the drying area.

Problems in Throwing off the Wheel Head

Many of the problems encountered when throwing off the wheel head are similar to those of throwing off the mound. There are, however, a few different ones, too. First, as we mentioned before, it is safer to have the wheel at a slower speed when working off the head, because it is difficult to control the larger amounts of clay.

Second, if you do not use a bat, removal of the pot from the wheel head can cause trouble, particularly if the clay is soft. Before cutting the pot loose from the wheel head, moisten the head with water or slip. Place a bat at the side of the wheel and, using even pressure, slide the pot across the moistened wheel head onto the bat.

If the clay is firm, place the hands as low as possible on the pot and, without squeezing or causing distortion, exert an even pressure from the fingertips to the heels of the hands to twist the pot slightly. When it has been released, lift. Be sure to have a bat close by on which to place the pot.

Fig. 107. Vase (10 inches tall) decorated with eucalyptus pods that were stamped on when clay was leatherhard. Iron oxide was rubbed in and sponged off all but the stamped areas. Flat matte glaze.

Fig. 108. Set of three canisters by Steve O'Loughlin, from 7 to 10 inches in height. Straight lids were made using technique described in Fig. 124. Sgraffito design. Rims have been dipped in a second glaze.

Fig. 109. Wheel-thrown light sculpture made from two basic forms—cylinder and bowl—in combination with plexiglass tubing. Height: 11 inches. Top of the lower section has a dark fluid glaze over the first glaze.

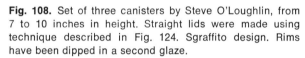

MAKING A LARGE BOTTLE

The bottle is a variation of the basic cylinder shape. The desired oval or spherical form of the lower part of the bottle is achieved by exerting pressure with the left hand from the inside outward at the widest point, the right hand always used to oppose the pressure of the left. After the desired shape has been achieved, the neck and top are completed as follows:

Fig. 110. Collar in over a large area, using both hands on the clay and lifting up as you apply pressure toward the center.

Fig. 111. Thin the top by pinching the clay with the left hand and pushing in and lifting up with the right.

Fig. 112. Shape the neck by pushing in with the right hand against the left. Gradually push in and lift up.

Fig. 113. Finish the neck as for the small bottle. To finish the base, hold a trimming spear or wood tool firmly with both hands and, following the curve of the pot, cut slowly toward the bat. It may take two or three trims to achieve the desired shape. Undercutting too rapidly or too deeply will collapse the pot.

Fig. 114. Peel off the trim ring. After some experience, you will be able to trim so well that you will not need to do further trimming at the base during the separate trimming process later (see Figs. 129 to 133). When the finishing is complete, use a nylon clay cutter to release the pot from the bat.

Fig. 115. Two bottle shapes of a size (8 inches and 10 inches) that can be thrown off the wheel head or bat. Several glazes have been overlaid to get a multicolored effect.

THE BOWL: BASIC PROCESSES

Throwing a bowl off the head differs from throwing one off the mound primarily in the amount of clay used. The centering and opening processes are the same as for the cylinder with one difference: the bowl is centered wide and slightly flat. As a result, it does not have to be pulled or opened at the base quite so much as the cylinder in order to achieve the desired width.

Centering and Opening

Fig. 116. Center clay wide and flat.

Lifting and Shaping

Fig. 117. Lift with the fingers opposite each other, the right hand outside the walls, the left inside. Lift and pull toward you with the left hand, pushing with the right hand to control the shape. The fingers should be firmly fixed together, the wheel at a slow speed.

Fig. 118. Continue pulling and lifting, flaring the wall with careful pressure, until the bowl is the desired shape. Do not pull the wall too far off the vertical or it will collapse. Note the width of the base in relation to the width at the rim.

Fig. 119. Complete the shaping of the inside of the bowl with a finishing rubber or bowl rib, keeping the right hand on the outside to exert gentle pressure against the left hand. Excessive shaping outward will cause bowl to collapse.

Fig. 120. Compress the rim by pressing in toward the center and clean it with a sponge or piece of chamois.

Fig. 121. Set of stacked mixing bowls, 4½ to 8 inches high, by Steve O'Loughlin. Clay for all three was measured out before beginning the throwing.

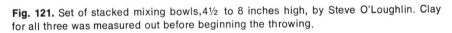

CASSEROLES: RIMS AND LIDS

Casseroles are made exactly like bowls through the lifting process, but may differ from the uncovered bowl in the finishing process, depending on the type of lid that is desired. The simplest rim to make is a plain one—slightly flared—into which the lid can be set. The process for rim and lid is essentially the same as that for jar and lid, discussed in Chapter 4, Figs. 67 to 71.

Another type of rim is the ledged rim, into which a domed lid can be set. The ledged rim is commonly used on glass casseroles, which you probably have in your home. The following illustrations describe the making of the ledged rim and the domed lid.

Fig. 122. For a ledged rim, the rim of the pot should be left thick, at least ½ inch. Using a straight-edged tool, such as the putty knife shown here, split the rim with the corner of the knife, angling downward toward the center to create the flat ledge. The pressure must be *slow,* with the wheel turning moderately fast. Problems occur when the pushing is so fast that the rim is forced off center, or when the rim is uneven in thickness or height.

Fig. 123. The domed lid can be made for either the straight or the ledged rim. The mound for the domed lid should be centered flat and wide. To open, pull across with the thumb of the right hand against the restraining pressure from the left. The opening should be slow, with the wheel turning moderately fast. Make sure the right arm is firmly braced.

Fig. 124. If the casserole rim is plain and straight, the rim of the lid should be shaped with a straight-edged tool so that the inner lip fits inside the rim of the casserole, the outer lip extending slightly. If the casserole rim has a ledged lip, the inner lip on the lid may be omitted.

Fig. 125. Before the lid is released from the bat, trim off excess clay at the base with a turning tool. When the lid is leatherhard, invert, center, and trim round or domelike. Then apply handle.

Fig. 126. Two types of casseroles, both 6 inches high with 2-quart capacity. *Left:* Set-in lid was thrown on a bat right side up. Rim on casserole is flared out, without a ledge. Handles have been attached for ease in carrying while hot. Combed design was cut through wet iron slip while pot was still on the wheel. (By Jay Trenchard.) *Right:* Domed lid was thrown upside down, much like a shallow bowl, then turned over and trimmed round when leatherhard. Pulled handle was attached at the same time. Casserole has a ledged rim.

Fig. 127. Fondue pots by Steve O'Loughlin. Bases of pots rest in flared rims of separate candle warmers. Handles were thrown like goblet stems. *Left:* Glaze is a combination of two matte glazes—red and yellow. Height: 9 inches. *Right:* Blue gloss glaze over carved design, with two glazes overlaid on base glaze. Height: 7½ inches. Glaze on rim of candle warmers requires that they be fired separately from pots.

Fig. 128. Covered jar, 7 inches high. Lid is bowl-shaped, with two holes punched through for macramé handle, which carries out the motif of the band design on the jar. Jar rim has ledge. Matte glaze over wax-resist oxide design.

TRIMMING

After the pot is leatherhard, it is returned to the wheel for the final process of trimming, at which time irregularities—such as a base that is overly thick or not level—can be corrected and the foot of the pot finished. As mentioned at the end of the sequence on making a large bottle, the experienced potter is able to shape the outside base of the pot as the last step before the pot is removed from the wheel. For the beginning potter, however, there will normally be need for considerable shaping at the base during the trimming.

Bowls and bottles are trimmed in the same way, but they are affixed to the wheel head differently. The bowl is placed upside down on the head, centered, and anchored into place with either a coil of clay that is placed snugly around the pot and pressed firmly against the head or with four pieces of clay positioned as in Fig. 129. Bottles are inverted and anchored in a chuck, a thick cylinder thrown for the express purpose of holding the bottle (see Fig. 130).

If several bottles are to be trimmed, the size and shape of the chuck can be adjusted to accommodate each of them. The inside of the chuck should be lined with paper toweling to prevent the leatherhard bottles from sticking to the damp clay. After the trimming has been completed, the chuck itself can be thrown into a pot. In this case it is important to check that no leatherhard pieces of clay trimmings have gotten inside the cylinder.

Some potters prefer to use premade and prefired chucks of various sizes, and thus to avoid the need for throwing a cylinder each time they wish to trim a bottle. Since the chuck must be perfectly round if the trimming is to be even, there is some advantage to having a supply of premade chucks that have been tested for exact roundness. Chucks are fixed on the wheel head with clay in the same way as bowls. The upside-down bottle is anchored to the prefired chuck with coils of clay to prevent the bottle from moving while it is being trimmed.

Fig. 129.   Center the upside-down bowl and anchor it with pieces of clay pressed against the wheel head.

Fig. 130.   To trim a large bottle, use a thick cylinder (chuck) slightly flared at the top.

The trimming process is illustrated on a bottle in the chuck shown in Fig. 130. A considerable amount of clay has already been removed from the edge.

Fig. 131.   Before cutting the foot, consider the shape of the pot and determine what size foot or shape base will be attractive. Use a wire loop tool to trim slowly and carefully from the outside edge, turning the wheel moderately fast. Shape the foot as desired.

Fig. 132.   Before starting to trim the bottom, check the thickness of the base with a needle to determine the amount to be cut out. Starting at the center and moving outward, hollow out the bottom, leaving a circular foot about ¼ inch wide.

Fig. 133. The finished foot. Depending on the size of the pot, the hollowed out section will be from ⅛ to 3/16 inch deep.

THE PITCHER: SPOUT AND HANDLE

The pitcher is a cylinder shape to which are added a spout and a handle.

Fig. 134.   To make a spout, lightly pinch a portion of the rim between the left thumb and forefinger, forming a V, and use the right forefinger to pull the clay out—*once only*—between the V.

The handle should be applied to a pot only after the pot has been dried to the leatherhard stage or at least sufficiently to permit it to be worked without distorting its shape. The handle is an integral part of the total design of the pot and should be shaped for appearance as well as utility. The size of the handle should be appropriate to the size of the pot.

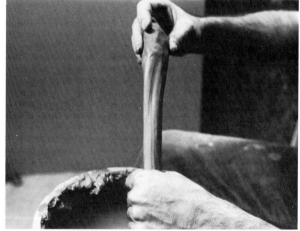

Fig. 135.   Begin with a coil of clay somewhat larger at one end than the other. Hold the large end with one hand; with the other hand, wetted, draw the clay downward with gentle, squeezing motions. Too much downward pull will break the clay; too little will accomplish nothing. Rotate the clay slightly as you draw it downward.

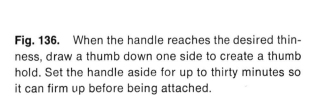

Fig. 136.   When the handle reaches the desired thinness, draw a thumb down one side to create a thumb hold. Set the handle aside for up to thirty minutes so it can firm up before being attached.

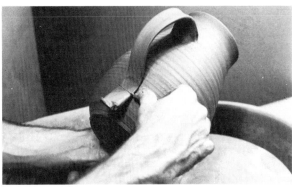

Fig. 137. After cutting off the bulb of clay at the top, determine the spots on the pot where the top and bottom of the handle will be placed. (The handle must be directly across from the spout. See Fig. 142 for line guides.) Score these places and wet them. Wait a few minutes.

Fig. 138. Slightly score the top of the handle where it is to join the pot and apply it by pushing the clay against the scored spot on the pot, holding one hand inside the pot to prevent distortion.

Fig. 139. Slightly score bottom of shaped handle at point of juncture; apply to the lower scored spot on pot. Cut off any excess clay. Smooth out both joints.

Fig. 140. Soup tureen, 7 inches high, 2½ quart capacity; ladle; and tray. Tray was made flat on the bat with only a slight flare, left to dry before being cut off the wheel head underneath, and then removed and trimmed. Ladle, by Freeman Loughridge, is a combination of a small bowl with a spout and a pulled handle. Yellow tan matte glaze with overlaid contrasting glazes. Underside of ladle handle at tip end and point where ladle bowl rests have been left unglazed so that the ladle can be fired without sticking to the kiln shelf.

Fig. 141. Examples of utilitarian pottery, by Steve O'Loughlin, made in sets. Cups (3½ inches high) were thrown off the mound, the same amount of clay centered each time, thereby assuring the experienced potter cups of the same size. Clay for the bat-thrown plates (diameter: 8 inches) should be measured or weighed to assure uniformity. Individuality of design comes from varying the glaze patterns so that no two pieces in a set are exactly alike.

MAKING AND USING LINE GUIDES

Hanging pots and planters (see Fig. 143) are normally suspended by three ropes or thongs fastened through holes or handlelike lugs attached to the pots. The holes must be precisely 120 degrees apart if the pot is to hang evenly. You will need a device of some kind to locate the precise points on the pots where the holes should be made. You can make a simple line guide (see Fig. 142) by stapling the ends of three equal lengths of construction board or heavy paper together, or you can make a more detailed guide as follows:

Starting with construction board or heavy paper, cut out a rectangle or square approximately 12 inches across. Locate the center by drawing light diagonal lines. With a compass and either lead pencil or waterproof ink, inscribe concentric circles half an inch apart. Then, using a protractor, draw lines 120 degrees apart, extending from the center to the edge. Cut the guide around the largest circle and use an acrylic matte varnish on the surface to make it water resistant.

When you invert a bowl on the guide, center it by making sure that its circumference is uniformly distant from the nearest circle. The three lines will indicate where the holes should be made.

By drawing a straight line across the guide through the center, you will be shown where two holes or designs should be made. In making a pitcher the guide assures that the handle is directly across from the spout.

Mark the lines in some way (an "X" is used on the sample) to indicate which lines form a triangle as distinct from the straight line.

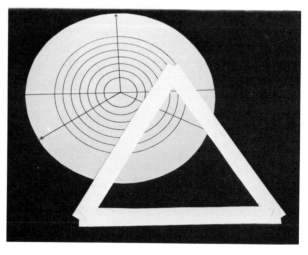

Fig. 142. Line guides for aligning holes in hanging planters and other pots.

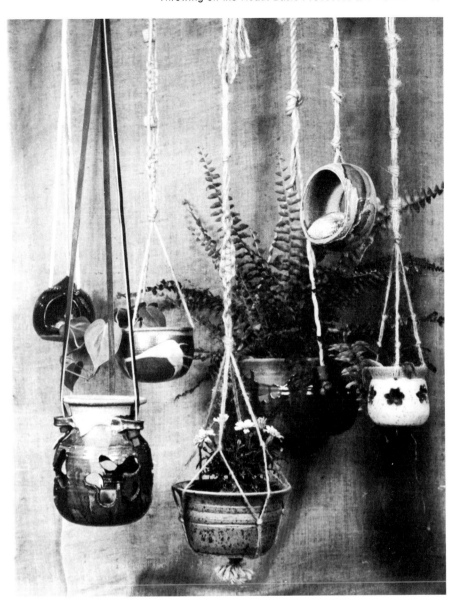

Fig. 143. Hanging pots thrown off the wheel head or mound, ranging from 4 to 10 inches in height. *Left to right:* (1) Small bird feeder, by Freeman Loughridge, with splashed glaze, light over dark. (2) Large candle holder with leather straps. Open areas were cut out with a needle, pushed through the clay to the hilt, and moved slowly when the clay was leatherhard. (3) Small planter with macramé hanger, by Judy Howell, also showing splash technique. (4) Large planter with indented line design and macramé sling. (5) Large planter with lugs to hold rope. Lugs can be pulled, cut with a handle maker, or cut in 1-inch-wide sections from a thrown cylinder. Unbraided part of rope must be tied off to prevent further unbraiding. (6) Bird feeder, by Judy Howell. An upended, open, slightly oval cylinder, with holes cut in top for the rope. Oval effect was achieved by making cylinder just thin enough to permit a slight collapse when removing. (7) Small candle holder with macramé hanger.

SUMMARY

Basic Forms off the Head

Cylinder: Vase

1. Begin as for centering off the mound, the left hand pushing, the right hand pulling.
2. Push clay down into flat mound.
3. Contain clay with both hands, pushing and pulling to center.
4. With arms braced, begin opening with thumbs.
5. Complete opening with fingers of left hand inside, the right hand bracing on the outside.
6. Pull across with left hand into right hand.
7. Collar in to straighten up sides.
8. Shift body position to right side, with right arm locked into hip.
9. With hands rigid, lift the clay with balls of fingers spread over a broad area of the clay. Use sponge if necessary. Left fingers are inside the pot.
10. Complete lifting using opposing pressure of fingertips. Left hand is inside cylinder, slightly above right hand outside cylinder. Thin walls to desired thickness.
11. Begin shaping at base, left hand pressing against right hand.
12. Trim.
13. Complete shaping by collaring in top with both hands.
14. Remove.

Bottle

1. Center and open as for a cylinder base, but leave rim heavier.
2. Collar in with both hands over a broad area, lifting at the same time.
3. Thin top by pinching with left hand and lifting with right.
4. Shape neck by pushing in with right hand against left, gradually lifting at the same time.
5. Finish rim with fingertips.
6. Trim and remove.

Bowl

1. Center clay wide and flat.
2. Open as for a cylinder.
3. With wheel at slow speed, lift and pull out, using almost equal pressure from both hands. Left hand is inside, right hand outside.
4. Shape from inside with bowl rib. Control shape with right hand.
5. Compress rim by pressing in toward center.
6. Trim and remove.

6

Hand-building

Shaping clay by hand is the most ancient method of making pottery. The development of the potter's wheel facilitated the making of round, symmetrical forms but was nevertheless not essential, since all forms that can be made on the wheel can also be made by hand, though perhaps not with the same perfection. Hand-building has the advantage of permitting the construction of countless forms not possible on the wheel. The potter using the techniques of hand-building is not limited to round shapes, and consequently the possibilities of individualistic design are increased. Hand-building, in fact, leads the potter into the realm of sculpture.

The three basic methods of hand-building are pinching, coiling, and the use of clay slabs. Like throwing, the pinch method involves the shaping of a form from a single lump of clay, but the other two methods require the joining of clay to clay. It is this difference—apart from the potentialities of design— that must be the chief consideration in shaping by hand. The strength of the joints is of great importance; like a chain, a hand-built pot is no stronger than its weakest joint, and the most carefully and imaginatively designed pot is a failure if it falls apart during the drying or firing stage.

Some fundamental points about joining should be kept in mind. In the coil method, clay joins to clay as the coil builds upward, and normally all the clay is wet enough to join easily. When slabs are used, however, they are generally not joined until they are close to leatherhard, in which case the surfaces to be joined must be scored. Scoring is the process of roughening two edges to be joined.

Successful hand-building depends to a great degree upon the consistency of the clay. It is best to use a clay with moderate to heavy amounts of grog to give strength to the pots as they are being constructed. The clay must be firm enough to stand up —to hold its shape—and at the same time wet enough to permit strong, cohesive joints. The potter who has begun on the wheel will have developed a feel for clay and will know when the clay is too stiff, too soft, or of the proper consistency for shaping by hand. For the potter who begins with hand-building, it will be necessary to develop this instinct for the feel of clay. Either way, it is perhaps best to begin hand-building with the pinch method, which permits the most direct and sustained contact between the hands and the clay.

Thorough and careful drying before firing is important with all pottery, but especially with hand-built pots. They are often thicker than thrown pots, and because of the joints or seams, there is a greater possibility of irregular thickness with such pots. If care is not taken to assure slow, equal drying, the outer surface will dry more quickly than the inner surface, and the resulting shrinkage of the outer clay will cause cracking. When slip has been added to the joints, the water in the clay will be unevenly distributed and will need some time to equalize. Wrapping the pot in plastic and allowing it to stand for several days will permit the necessary equalizing of the moisture throughout the clay.

The drying process must be unhurried. Clay of any thickness, within reason, can be fired without exploding ("blowing") or breaking if it is thoroughly dry and the thickness is approximately the same throughout the object. It must be remembered that even after the air-drying process there is still "chemical water" in the clay that must escape as the clay vitrifies under intense heat. Cracking will result if the firing is too rapid to permit the water to escape evenly throughout.

Although air drying is the best course to follow, the drying process may be speeded up by placing pots in an oven at a low temperature after they have become leatherhard. Forced drying is risky, however, and is not recommended. Nor should new greenware (unfired pottery) be placed in the sun to hurry the drying, since uneven drying and subsequent cracking are the inevitable results.

The thickness of a hand-built pot should be in proportion to the size of the pot. A small pot may be less than ¼ inch thick; a large pot several feet high can have walls of ¾ inch thickness. A pot *should* weigh what it looks as if it should weigh; that is, anyone picking it up expects to feel a certain heaviness, based upon previous experience with other objects of similar size and shape. If the pot does not conform to this expectation, it is poorly constructed.

Similarly, the decoration of a hand-built pot depends upon its shape and size as well as on the objective of the potter. Hand-built constructions lend themselves to a variety of decorative techniques. Not only can they be carved with the regular tools of the potter, but all types of organic and inorganic objects —pieces of wood, nut shells, fruit pits, leaves, pine cones, rope, forks, combs, gears—may be used to create designs that both individualize the pot and complement its size and shape.

PINCHING

In the hands of the potter, a ball of plastic clay that fits easily into the palm of the hand can be pinched into numerous forms that are utilitarian— such as small bowls for nuts and candies—or decorative. The clay used for pinching should have some grog for strength and be of the proper consistency for comfortable shaping by hand without the addition of water. The hands must be dry when making a pinch pot; if not, the clay will become too moist to hold its shape.

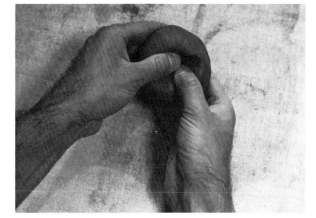

Fig. 144.   Roll a lump of clay into a ball and depress the center with the thumbs, keeping the fingers tightly together underneath the ball. Rotate the ball as you depress the thumbs and open the ball deeply, taking care not to flatten it out.

Fig. 145.   Proceed with the pinching until the clay is about as thin as you wish. The pinching lifts and pushes the clay from the opening to form the walls. A thickness of about ¼ inch is best for small pinch pots. The thickness should be even throughout.

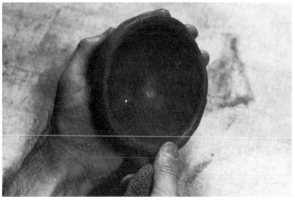

Fig. 146.   Finish the surface using the thumb and, if necessary, a sponge on the inside surface. The pot may be slightly uneven and have finger marks on it, but these characteristics are traditional for pinch pots. To flatten the bottom so the pot will sit level, gently tap the pot on a flat surface.

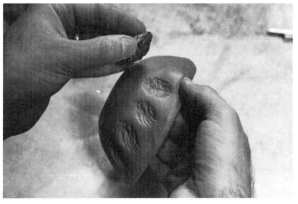

Fig. 147.   Decorate the pot to your taste. Experiment with a variety of objects, but keep each pot simple in design.

PINCHING PROBLEMS

Fig 148. The bottom of this pinch pot cracked because drying was too rapid. Cracking can also result from walls of uneven thickness.

Fig. 149. These finished pinch pots, heavily textured and carved, some with pinched edges, reveal by their appearance their hand-built origin; such pots could not be made on the wheel. The three small pots, all made by the method described in the preceding sequence, are joined in a triangle. The pot on the right was made by joining two oval-shaped pots and puncturing and squeezing in the pot on top. A nail point was used for the incised decoration. The rear pot was also made from two oval-shaped pots, the top one then punctured and the lip pinched and smoothed. The decoration was achieved by grating leatherhard clay and applying it to the plastic surface with the fingers. When two pots are joined into a spherical form, the ball must be punctured to permit air to escape during drying and firing.

COILING

Like pinching, coiling is an ancient method of making pottery, but to the primitive potter it provided a great step forward, for it permitted the creation of large containers. Coiling is the process of making a pot by adding either separate coil rings or long, spiraling coils to a base. The technique lends itself to the making of either small pots such as can be thrown on a wheel, or larger pots that wheel throwing cannot handle. The shapes possible with coiling are almost endless, but its best use is perhaps for off-round, oval, or free-form sculptured shapes and for effects not possible on the wheel.

The underside of oilcloth proves a good working surface for coiling, for clay does not adhere to it. Since coiling requires frequent movement of the pot under construction, it is advisable, especially with larger pots, to work off a bat or other movable surface or to use a modeling wheel. Almost any clay may be used for coiling, but it should be both plastic enough for comfortable shaping and firm enough to hold its shape without excessive stretching.

Making a Base

Bases can be made in a variety of ways. A ball of clay can be pressed out flat—about ⅜ inch thick for a pot of 6 to 10 inches high—into a shape slightly larger than the base needed. Taller pots need proportionately thicker bases. If a circular base is desired, an indentation may be made with a round object of the desired size, and then the clay base cut out with a needle. If a modeling wheel is used, the needle may be held firmly at the appropriate point on the diameter and a line scored through as the wheel is turned. Or the base may be fashioned from a strip of the clay that has been rolled out for coiling. In this case the strip of clay is coiled around itself until a base of the desired size is achieved. The joints are smoothed over as the base is enlarged. If a free-form, curvilinear shape is wanted for the base, it can be drawn freehand or traced from a design on a flat piece of pressed clay. Fig. 150 shows a base being made from a piece of pressed clay, with a small pot used to outline the circle that will be cut out with a needle. The completed base, ready for the coiling, is shown in Fig. 151.

Fig. 150. A circular base for a coil pot may be made in several ways. Here a small pot is used to outline a circle that will be cut out.

Making a Coil Pot

Fig. 151. Press out a lump of clay into a rough strip. (Note the base, ready for the coils to be attached.)

Fig. 152. Using only a slight pressure, and starting at the center, begin rolling the rough strip into an even strip. Keep fingers together to avoid finger depressions.

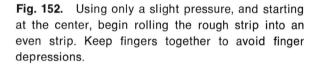

Fig. 153. As the clay strip stretches and lengthens, move your hands apart to control the clay. Keep pressure of hands even to avoid thick and thin spots. The length of the strip rolled out is limited only by the amount of clay you can adequately control. The diameter of coil will be about one-third to one-half thicker than the wall of finished pot, for pressing and joining the coils will reduce their thickness. Before beginning to make the pot you will need to make several strips of clay. Avoid excessive rolling, for your hands will dry the surface of the clay. Use the coils as soon as possible, before further drying prevents good seals between them.

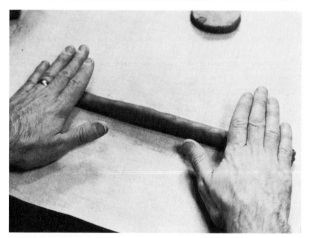

Fig. 154. To prepare the base for the first coil, score the base around the top edge and moisten with a small amount of water.

Fig. 155. Place the first length of clay around the scored base and attach it by pressing it down from the inside. (See Fig. 156 for butting process.) Each succeeding coil should be joined to the one under it in the same manner. Coils can be added as joined strands spiraling upward or as separate rings—for this pot separate rings are being used. At this point, join the rings inside by smoothing the clay to fill in spaces. After a few coils have been added, the pot should be allowed to stiffen and strengthen before adding more coils. This precaution will prevent sagging or collapsing.

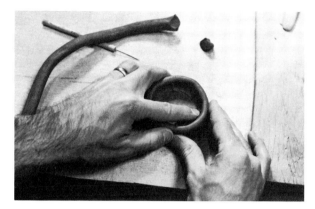

Fig. 156. Butt ends by scoring and pressing together firmly, then smoothing over so the joint does not show. If rings are used, take care that the butt ends are staggered, never placed one right above the other.

Fig. 157. Shape the pot as it rises by controlling the size of the rings or the spiraling coil. Smooth the outer surface with a wood rib or flexible metal rib— or leave the coils showing. This pot can be left as it is, with the top rings exposed as coils, or smoothed all over.

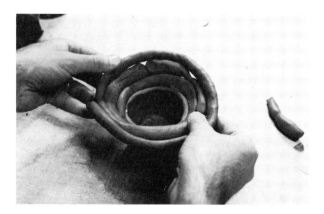

Coiling Problems

Fig. 158. This construction illustrates several problems: gaps caused by uneven thickness, failure to butt ends, failure to join the coils together by smoothing inside, and walls that flare so greatly they will not support the weight of the clay.

Fig. 159. These coil pots all have features that cannot be achieved on the wheel. *Left:* The coils were joined almost to the top, then two wheel-thrown spouts were added. Bottom section is heavily rubbed with red-iron oxides, the spouts finished with a brown matte glaze. *Center:* Asymmetrical jug with off-center spout; brown matte and white stony matte glazes. *Right:* The two pots show coils up-ended and circular to add variety. *On block, rear:* Iron oxide painted on and rubbed off with sponge, leaving iron in seams; glazed with matte glaze, which was also rubbed off to highlight coils. *Bottom:* Turquoise matte glaze.

Fig. 160. Sculptured bottles made with coils. Shapes should be developed as pots are built upward, not by adding or removing clay later. Surfaces were textured lightly with a palette knife and fired unglazed.

Fig. 161. Coils were pressed into a mold to give a controlled surface and mounted on a wheel-thrown base. Wires were glued into holes around the edge, the feathers glued onto the wires. The ceramics section is about 13 inches high.

SLAB CONSTRUCTIONS

The use of slabs permits the construction of an endless variety of pots and sculptured forms with rectangular or cylindrical walls. As with other types of hand-building, the use of slabs should be reserved for forms that cannot be wheel thrown, though spouts, lids, and other decorative attachments made on the wheel often can be employed with striking effects in combination with slabs.

Since slab constructions, like coiling, require clay to be joined to clay, the importance of strong joints cannot be overemphasized. The three principal types of joints used in slab work are butting, diagonal cutting, and pinching. Butted ends are used on flat surfaces that meet at right angles. Diagonal cuts, with overlapping edges, are useful for joining slabs to make oval or circular shapes, but may also be used instead of butted ends at right-angle joints. In this case the diagonal cuts are similar to beveled joints in woodworking. Pinched joints provide clear evidence of hand construction and can add dramatic effects to contrast with smooth slab walls. Except for pinched joints, all joints must be thoroughly scored and coated with slip.

The clay used for slab work can be any type that is not too finely grained. (Finely grained clay tends to warp during firing but it can be conditioned for slab use by the addition of twenty- to forty-mesh grog.) After slab pieces have been rolled and cut to the desired size and shape, they must be left to dry until firm but not quite leatherhard before being handled.

Fig. 162. The basic tools for slab constructions include two boards of about ⅜ inch thickness, rolling pin, ruler, pencil, scissors, steel rib, finishing rubber, needle, wood knife, sponge, and clay cutter. Also shown here are the basic joints used in slab work: diagonal joint used in round constructions, butted and diagonal joints used for 90 degree seams, and pinched joint. The diagonal joint is more trouble than the butted joint, but has the advantage of greater strength because more clay surface is joined.

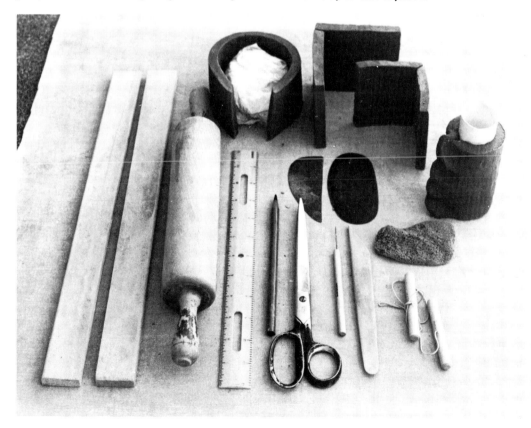

Making a Slab Box

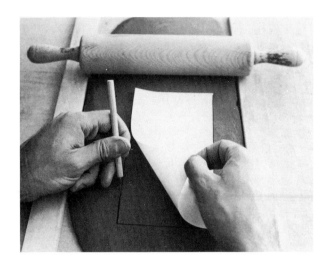

Fig. 163.   Use a rolling pin to roll out clay between boards of equal thickness, about ⅜ inch. Here common doorstop is being used. Take care to achieve even thickness throughout the slab. Pressure on the rolling pin must be firm, but not so hard as to cause the clay to adhere to the rolling pin and tear. After the slab has been rolled out, with a needle trace around a piece of paper cut to the desired size, and cut out the shape after the paper template has been removed.

Fig. 164.   When all the pieces for the construction have been cut out and are near leatherhard, lay them in position for joining. Score all the edges that will be joined. Some of the pieces will be scored on the side, as shown, and some on the edge. Check carefully to be certain that all necessary scoring is done. (Note the crosshatching of the scored areas.)

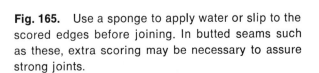

Fig. 165.   Use a sponge to apply water or slip to the scored edges before joining. In butted seams such as these, extra scoring may be necessary to assure strong joints.

Fig. 166. Join inside pieces first, twisting slightly as you press down to get a firm seal.

Fig. 167. Press outside pieces on firmly without altering shape of the box. Seal the joints inside the box with a wood tool.

Fig. 168. Roll out a small coil in your hand and apply to the inside corners and seams to strengthen the joints. Smooth the joints with a wood tool.

Making a Slab Cylinder

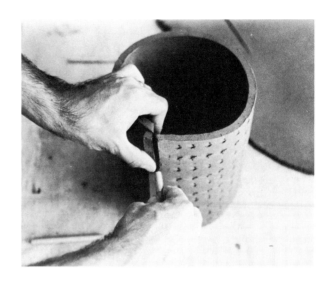

Fig. 169.   The walls of this cylinder are constructed from a continuous slab. To join, overlap the ends of the slab and cut through both sections with a needle in one long diagonal cut. Moisten edges with slip and join. The texture on the outside walls is achieved with the splintered end of a broken piece of wood.

Fig. 170.   After the cylinder has been seamed and smoothed, turn it upside down so that the foot can be joined to the base. Take care to score and use slip wherever joints are made.

   The lid, alongside the pot, was cut from a template matching the oval base, and the rim of the lid applied the same way as the foot.

Fig. 171.   The foot must be attached with care, for undue pressure will collapse the base. Use generous amounts of slip. Check to see that the foot is level and centered. Let dry slowly under plastic in this position.

Fig. 172. Slab box, used as planter, and cylinder shown in the previous sequence. Box was decorated by stamping with a eucalyptus pod and glazed with speckled satin matte. Handle was added to cylinder lid; glazed with rusty matte.

Fig. 173. Wall sculpture, 12 inches by 30 inches, made from slabs pressed over corrugated cardboard and then torn into smaller pieces. Pieces were joined in four separated sections by pinching over a paper mold. The sections were then joined with leather thongs, through holes at ends of the sections. Spouts are wheel-thrown bottle necks. Sculpture was nailed to board base with rusted nails.

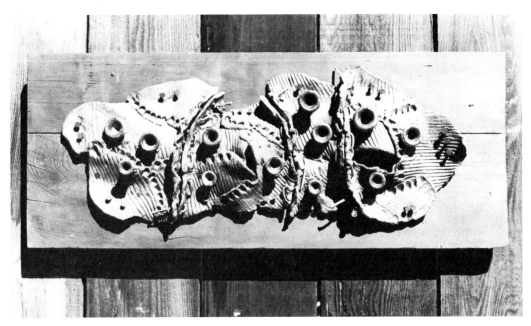

Fig. 174. *Left:* Weed pot, 9 inches high, for mounting on wall. Made from two slabs with pinched edges. Clay must be relatively soft to allow for pinching slab edges successfully. Crumpled paper toweling was placed inside pot during shaping so that sides would not collapse. *Center:* Slab pot, 11 inches tall, made around a wrapping paper tube and sealed by pinching. Top was wheel thrown. Decoration on side is small round slab with pinched edges, attached with slip. *Right:* Slab pot, 9½ inches tall, made from single slab with pinched seam. Texture on bottom section was achieved by rolling clay over crumpled paper. Neck was wheel thrown and pinched to slab walls.

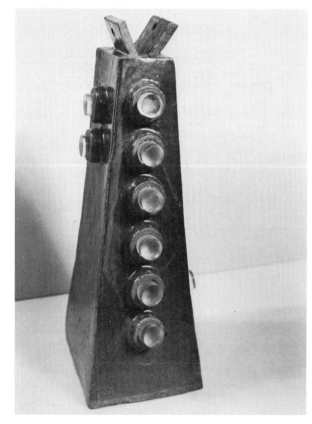

Fig. 175. Slab light sculpture, 15½ inches tall, with butted seams. Rings around plexiglass lights were cut from clay tubes made by wrapping slabs around a handmade cardboard tube. Lights were cut ½ inch long and cemented inside rings. Hole in base (not shown) allows for mounting a 25-watt bulb. Plexiglass tubes are available in various diameters, and can be cut with a fine saw into sections and smoothed with fine sandpaper. Clay rings into which plexiglass tubes are inserted must be made somewhat larger than the tubes to allow for shrinkage during drying and firing.

7

Design. Decoration. and Glazing

DESIGN AND DECORATION

Since pottery creations are both two and three dimensional, it is important to know the principles of design applying to both sculpture and surface decoration. In this chapter, taking up design, decoration, and glazing, we will deal with some aesthetic effects that complement a pot's form or function, and others, like glazing, that are at the same time decorative and functional.

STRUCTURAL DESIGN

Whereas certain art forms have an appeal that is essentially aesthetic or decorative, pottery constructions frequently combine aesthetic appeal with function. A pot intended for use as a pitcher, for example, should have the features necessary for a pitcher: the size appropriate to its purpose; a weight proportionate to its size and comfortable for lifting when pot is filled with liquid; a strong and serviceable handle; a spout that permits pouring without dripping; and a mouth sufficiently wide to permit easy filling and cleansing. The design must conform to these specifications. Similarly, vases, jars, bottles, cups, bowls, casseroles—all functional forms of pottery—have uses that impose requirements on design, and the potter is free to invent and create within these limits. However, even if the pot is intended as purely decorative, the structural design should conform within reasonable limits to the functional requirements of the basic form being used.

A major aesthetic decision in the structural design of a pot involves the relationship between the material being used—the clay—and the space surrounded by the clay. The space actually occupied by the clay is called positive space and relates to the size, shape, and contours of the pot. An object including handles and recesses has a clearly defined negative space, which is the hollow space that is surrounded by the clay. Negative space also refers, however, to the empty spaces that may not be enclosed by solids but that are merely suggested: for example, in a bottle, the space implied by the curve of the neck, or, in a goblet, the space between the bottom of the cup and the mass of the stem. The design of the pot should reflect a sensitive awareness of the relationship between positive and negative space and the fusion of these spaces into a harmonious whole.

Fig. 176. Doughnut-ring sculpture, suggestive of water bottles made early in nineteenth-century America. Farmers slung these bottles over an arm, leaving their hands free for carrying tools. (For construction details, see page 112.)

Since most pots—functional and decorative—are intended to sit or hang, balance is of primary importance. Balance is both physical and visual. Physical balance means that the pot does not topple over when it is set down on a table or hang lopsided when suspended; visual balance means that the features of a pot—its base, body, spouts, handles, lip, and openings—harmonize as parts of a whole. The base must give the appearance of sufficient size and mass to support the body of the pot; the handles and spouts must be in proportion to its size and shape.

These principles of structural design may be seen in Fig. 176. The positive space of the spout and the base combines with the body, the ring, to offset the massive negative space both within the ring and implied by the curve between the bottom of the ring and the base. Without the spout the pot would be adversely dominated by the negative space. The spout also adds necessary balance to the pot in two other ways. Visually, it offsets the base, for without it the pot would appear too squat; and the suggestion of narrowing where the spout joins the ring balances the upward narrowing of the base. The position of the spout slightly to one side also gives the suggestion of functional use, even though this pot was designed to be purely decorative. (Pots of this type, incidentally, can be made to serve as carafes.) If the spout were directly in the middle of the ring, there would still be a suggestion of function, as with a bottle or vase, but the off-centered position adds an almost necessary variation to what would otherwise be unrelieved symmetry. Visual balance is also achieved through the size of the base. If it were narrower or higher, it would not give the appearance of having enough mass to support the body.

Two final and essential points: First, it is a good basic principle to strive for simplicity in both structural design and decoration. Select a basic shape or motif and make the design and decoration conform to this motif and its variations. Avoid the temptation to incorporate excessive and widely varied features of design and decoration in a single pot. Second, keep in mind the medium with which you are working. Strive to create objects that take advantage of the features and qualities of clay and that look as though they have been made of clay. Though different media may have certain things in common, each art or craft medium also has special qualities which lend themselves to particular and sometimes unique effects.

The special qualities of clay are its extreme plasticity as it is shaped by the potter's hands and its capability of being subjected to a wide variety of decorative techniques. In the past, these qualities were frequently exploited to produce pottery pieces that resembled wares made of other material. During the Liao dynasty in China, for example, much of the pottery frequently resembled metallic or leather objects. Saddle gourds were made to look like leather and even had seams like the leather prototypes. Some contemporary pottery creations, however, have been designed to look *exactly* like metallic or wood or leather objects—water faucets, tree limbs, suitcases—and even though these objects illustrate the potter's technical virtuosity, it is arguable whether such creations have enduring value as examples of the potter's art.

The choice of design, within the limits discussed, belongs finally to the potter. In terms of the arts and crafts generally, the intimacy between the artist and his medium—the artist's control over, and alliance with, his medium—seems more pronounced in pottery making than in any other art or craft. It is perhaps significant that through the years the terminology of pottery description has incorporated terms that are essentially organic—*feet, bodies, shoulders, necks, mouths, lips.* In some abstract way successful potters have a feeling about clay, its earth origin, and its capacity to endure the elements and time that is reflected in their creations. These feelings may constitute an ultimate principle of pottery design.

APPLIED DESIGN: DECORATION

Just as the function or implied function of a pot is a basic consideration in its structural design, so is the structural design a basic consideration in the choice of the applied design or decoration. All three elements—function, structure, and decoration—must work together as an integrated whole. The experienced potter will, in fact, keep all three elements in mind during the entire creative process, from the initial shaping of the clay to the last decorative application.

Glazing is the most common decorative technique, since it is also important functionally—enabling a pot to hold liquids and providing a smooth, washable surface. Because of its importance it is the subject of a major portion of this chapter. Before we get into glazing, however, let's first discuss some of the most basic principles of pottery decoration and illustrate some of the easier decorative methods.

As with structural design, simplicity should be the guiding principle in decoration. The best decoration is a restrained, repeated motif suitable to the structure of the pot. Combinations of motifs or overdecoration are likely to be fatal to the organic unity of a pot. (Study the photograph of mound-thrown pots in Chapter 4, Fig. 85; note the simple variations of a motif that are used for each of the pots.)

Let the structural design of the pot determine the decorative motif. A pot that is basically round, for example, does not normally lend itself well to sharp, angular decoration. The motif should be curvilinear. Angular motifs, on the other hand, are appropriate for angular structures. In looking at pots in museums you will probably find these principles violated and yet aesthetically pleasing. Like all design principles, they are not hard and fast, but they are useful for the beginning potter.

Nor should the motif be out of balance with the size of the structure. The design should not be so large as to obliterate or dominate the pot, nor so small as to fade into insignificance. The smaller the pot, the less dominant should be the decoration, and the larger the pot, the more the decoration may dominate without overpowering the pot.

Decoration may be used effectively to contrast with structural design. Vertical motifs, for example, may be used to make a short pot appear taller, and horizontal motifs will make a tall pot appear fuller. Decoration may be employed to add interest to an otherwise large and plain expanse. Effectively used, decoration can make a mundane pot look good and can make a good pot look truly great.

The decoration should be more than something added or applied after the pot has been made. If it is only an addition, it is likely to detract from the pot rather than enhance it.

Give thought to the intended decorative process as you shape the pot. After the pot is shaped, *look at it* from a distance. Consider its outline, its form, its positive and negative space, its balance. Choose a type of design you think will be handsome and experiment with it on pieces of scrap clay or, for wax or oxide decorations, on pieces of paper toweling, which has about the same absorption quality as clay. If the pot is rounded, try a rounded or curved design;

if it is straight, try a straight design. Draw an outline of the pot and sketch in various motifs to see which one you think is best looking. But do not experiment on the actual pot itself.

Decoration may be applied at any of several stages of pot making—when the pot is still wet and plastic, in a greenware state; when it is leatherhard or nearly so; or when it is dry or has been bisque fired. Decoration at the last stage will be explained under glazing. The following examples of decorative techniques are discussed according to pot stages. Most of the pots are shown both in process and in finished states.

Decorating Greenware

While still on the wheel, thrown greenware may be decorated using a variety of tools, including the fingers. Fig. 177 illustrates five basic techniques.

Fig. 177. *Left to right:*
Carving or incising. Line decoration was incised while pot was still a narrow cylinder. The design spread out as the pot was rounded out from inside, thereby giving the effect of having grown with the pot rather than being carved into it.

Pinching. Pinching was done with the right thumb and forefinger, while the fingers of left hand pushed out from inside the pot opposite each pinched area. The neck was collared in after pinching.

Slip trailing. The plastic container served as a squeeze bottle holding slip that was trailed on the shoulder of the pot and allowed to run naturally down the walls.

Brushing. Porcelain slip was brushed onto the pot in a wide band, then cut through to the dark clay with a decorating tool.

Pushing. While the pot was still in cylinder shape, random pokes from the inside were made with one finger. The neck was then collared in without distorting the decoration.

Fig. 178. Finished glazed pots decorated while wet. The second and third pots, both decorated with fingers, have been highlighted by the additional use of iron oxide and wax.

Decorating Leatherhard Clay

More forceful techniques must be used on leather-hard clay than on plastic clay. Figs. 179 and 180 illustrate several basic techniques.

Fig. 179. *Left to right:*

Carving. Incised lines were made with a decorating tool, starting narrow at the top and deepening and widening toward the base to conform to the shape of the pot.

Paddling. Pot was flattened on four sides, then paddled with the end of a stick to achieve a bursting effect.

Fig. 180. *Left to right:*

Wheel carving. Pot was anchored to the wheel head and then randomly incised as the wheel turned slowly.

Slab appliqué. Oval slab was cut up and then attached to heavily scored area with slip. Additional texture was given to slab by pressing it onto the pitcher with a piece of rough wood.

Stamping and carving. Two types of decoration were used to take advantage of the shape of the pot. A eucalyptus pod was pressed around the distinct shoulder, with rough vertical lines scored with a decorating tool beneath each of the pod impressions.

Fig. 181. Clay slip is painted onto leatherhard pitcher, then carved through with a wood tool.

Fig. 182. Finished, glazed pots decorated during leatherhard stage. *Left to right:* Leatherhard decorations were highlighted by (a) iron oxide under the glaze; (b) cobalt oxide over the glaze in the depressions; (c) wax on the slab appliqué; (d) wax on the horizontal band and iron oxide on the vertical lines.

Banding

Round pots may be returned to the wheel in either the leatherhard or bisque-fired stage for banding and brush applications of oxides or engobes.

Fig. 183. Load a Japanese brush with oxide or engobe and hold steadily in place as the wheel turns slowly. Oxides and carbonates of metals are the easiest to use for banding, but color possibilities are greater with colored clay slips or engobes.

Fig. 184. Zigzag banding should be somewhat free flowing. Do not try for precision. Move brush up and down as wheel turns slowly.

Fig. 185. Finished, glazed pot with banding, which has been highlighted by semitranslucent white glaze. Speckled effect is a feature of the clay, which has iron spots in it.

Decorating Examples

The pots illustrated in the following four photographs were decorated using some of the techniques just discussed, as well as others not described. They illustrate merely a few of the endless design techniques available, for clay is a receptive medium for stamped impressions and for carved, paddled, pushed, pulled, and appliquéd designs. The construction of some of the pots, made by joining smaller pieces, will be discussed in the next chapter.

Fig. 186. Heavy rope was crisscrossed around pot before leatherhard stage and carefully pressed and pulled in to create impressions without grossly distorting the pot. After bisque firing, rope impressions were rubbed with heavy iron oxide, which burned through the glaze during the glaze firing. Height: 10 inches.

Fig. 187. Vertical carved slab strips, applied on scored areas (front and back) in bas-relief, complement vertical thrust of pot. Slab strips were carved with free-form shapes and patterns and brushed with a matte glaze. Body of pot left unglazed. Height: 12 inches.

Fig. 188. Twisted, pulled handles add excitement to vase with simple, straight sides. Carved design is emphasized by application of iron oxide. Rim is dipped in darker glaze. Height: 10 inches. (By Robert L. Wolchock.)

Fig. 189. *Left:* Vertical lines carved during near leatherhard stage reinforce shape of pot. Counter effect was achieved by pressing small balls of clay onto scored areas and decorating them with a variety of objects, including a drinking straw, a film spool, a needle, twigs, and old jewelry. Unglazed body with dark brown glazed rim. Height: 12½ inches.
    Right: Random texture achieved by pressing scored areas during leatherhard stage with a needle and wheel trimmings of varying lengths and widths. Textured section left in natural clay. Top and bottom dipped into dark brown glaze after bisque firing. Height: 17½ inches. (See Chapter 8, p. 112, for construction.)

Fig. 193. Wax the rim of the lid, again leaving a ¼-inch safety margin.

If you wish to do any wax-resist decorating before the glaze is applied, it must also be done at this stage. The same wax used for the bottom can be used for decorating, using either a free design or banding (on the wheel) or both. Before applying the wax, practice the design on a paper towel, which has an absorption rate about the same as that of a bisque pot.

Fig. 194. Wax has been painted on the bisque pot to create a design. The unglazed clay will show through the waxed area when the pot is glazed and fired. (See Figs. 212, 213, 223, 230, and 232 for other pots decorated using the wax-resist technique.)

Glaze Mixing

Once you have selected a glaze, you should have a sufficient supply of it ready for your immediate needs. What constitutes a sufficient supply depends upon the size and number of pots you plan to glaze, but from two to five pounds (746 to 1,865 grams) of dry glaze will make a workable glaze batch. Figure that 1,000 grams of dry glaze will produce roughly a half gallon of wet glaze, which is about the minimum that can be used successfully. For mixing, you will need a container for each glaze. For most purposes, plastic containers (buckets, trash containers, wastebaskets) with capacities of from two quarts to six gallons will serve nicely. (If containers have no lids, make them of masonite or plywood. The lids will keep moisture from evaporating unnecessarily and will keep out impurities and splashings from other glazes.)

Lay out all of the materials and equipment necessary: the glaze powder, the mixing container, a pitcher (with a ready supply of water), an eighty-mesh sieve, and a tool for stirring. The stirring tool may be a restaurant-type mashed potato whisk, an electric drill with a paint-mixing attachment, or any paddle or implement that will serve for vigorous stirring (see Fig. 190).

Fig. 195. Add a small quantity of water to the mixing container.

Fig. 196. Add a quantity of the glaze powder.

Fig. 197.   Stir vigorously. Add more water and powder and stir until all of the powder is mixed in. Keep the mixture relatively heavy until all the dry glaze has been added. (If it is too thick, it can be thinned with water. If too thin, let glaze settle for several hours and scoop off the water from the top.) The glaze should have the consistency of thick cream.

Fig. 198.   Test the glaze for proper consistency by dipping a finger into it. The glaze should coat the finger evenly, without running off, and you should be able to see the outline of your fingernail through it. If glaze runs off your finger, it is too thin. If you draw your finger across the surface of the glaze and leave a trail, the glaze is generally too thick. To make certain that the glaze is smooth throughout, strain the mix through an eighty-mesh sieve to locate any large, unmixed particles that would otherwise mar the surface of the clay ware upon firing.

Not all glazes require the same thickness to attain the best results. Glossy glazes as a rule go on thinner than matte glazes. When glossy glazes are too thick, they tend to run during firing. You will have to try your glazes at different thicknesses and keep a record of the results.

When the glazed pot is dry, check the thickness of glaze by scratching with a needle at the bottom edge. If the glaze comes off in a big piece, it is too thick. To remove the excess glaze, sand it down with the thumb or finger to the desired thickness.

Since the liquid glaze mixture is composed of insoluble matter in a water suspension, it is necessary to stir it vigorously every few minutes as you use it so that it will not settle. Be sure that the bottom of the container contains no sediment and that the consistency is even throughout. Test frequently for consistency. This point cannot be overemphasized. Some of the greatest problems in glazing are caused by an inconsistent mixing or thickness of glaze, with sediment on the bottom and excess water at the top.

Not all the glaze will necessarily be used at one time. It should be kept in its container, carefully covered to prevent contaminants from getting into it, until it is needed again. Before it is re-used, however, water will probably have evaporated from it and will have to be added. And it must be carefully tested again for consistency.

Glaze Application

There are four principal methods for applying glaze: dipping, pouring, brushing, and spraying. For the beginner, the most successful results can be achieved with the first two methods. Brushing is particularly difficult because brush strokes invariably show, and it is almost impossible to get an even glaze coat with a brush. Spraying requires expensive equipment—a compressor, a sprayer, and (if used indoors) a spray booth with an exhaust fan. Moreover, it is very difficult to get an even thickness with a spray gun, and the fine powder from the spray is so delicate that it comes off very easily if touched. When a subtle change in shading or a fade-out in color is desired, spraying is a useful technique, but for the beginner the disadvantages far outweigh the advantages (see Fig. 211 for a pot glazed by spraying). Dipping and pouring are both relatively simple methods that can provide satisfying results.

Dipping

Dipping is a useful method when an ample supply of glaze is available. All the work may be done over the glaze container.

Fig. 199. Glaze the inside of the pot first. Fill it about half full of the glaze, rotating it carefully at a uniform rate so that the glaze does not adhere too thickly at one spot. Keep turning the pot until the entire inside is covered. Then quickly pour out the excess glaze.

Fig. 200. To glaze the outside, hold the pot on the rim and at the bottom and quickly submerge it, making certain that the opening is perfectly level so that the air pressure on the inside of the pot will prevent any glaze from entering it. Different glazes are used on the inside and outside of this pot.

Fig. 201. Remove the pot and shake off the excess glaze. Dab glaze on the rim where you held the pot. Sponge off any excess glaze from the bottom. Note the effect of the glaze on the scored and carved area treated with wax resist.

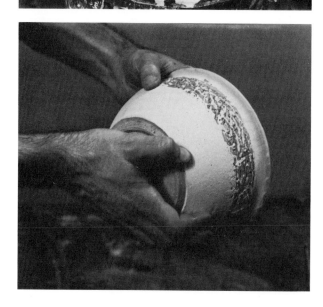

Fig. 202. After the glaze is dry, use light pressure of a finger or thumb to smooth any rough spots or spots where the glaze has run and become thick, especially near the base.

Pouring

When a lesser quantity of glaze is available, or if the container holding the glaze is smaller than the object being glazed, the pouring method should be used.

Fig. 203. Glaze the inside of the pot first, as with the dipping method.

Fig. 204. Hold the pot upside down over the container and quickly but evenly pour the glaze in a circular motion to cover the entire pot. Sponge off any glaze that has gotten on the bottom. Smooth out rough spots, as in Fig. 202.

Other Methods

After the initial glazing has been completed, other methods may be used to add decorative effects. One of the more common methods is banding, discussed earlier in Figs. 183 to 185. Banding may be done on either the bisque or the glazed pot.

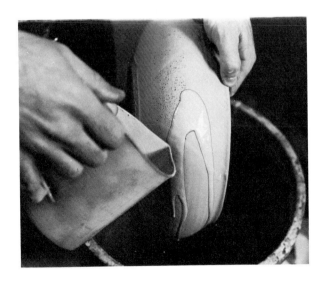

Fig. 205. *Splashing.* Use a small amount of different glaze in a small container for a glaze splash. Keep this second glaze from the edge or foot of the pot to prevent excessive thickness that might run during the firing.

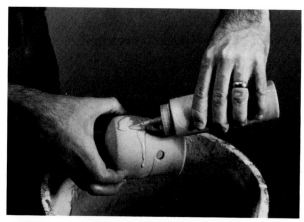

Fig. 206.   Use a squeeze bottle to attain a carefully controlled splash design.

Fig. 207.   *Using oxides.* An oxide can be painted on the glaze. The glaze should be very stable so as not to flow and obliterate the design.

Fig. 208. Finished, glazed pot showing slight flowing of the iron oxide. Carved bands have been decorated with glued-on leather strips. Height, including lid: 6½ inches.

Glazing Examples

The end results of several glazing techniques can be studied further in the following pictures.

Fig. 209. Asymmetrical, sculptured, two-gallon slab punch bowl, by Patricia Haeger, with distinctly different inside and outside glazes. The inside was glazed by pouring method with rutile glaze, and the outside by brushing with rutile glaze and then brushing over much of the rutile with a brown magnesium glaze. Outside sculptured effects were highlighted with other brushed glazes in rattan, brown, green, black, and white. Height: 8 inches; diameter: 10½ inches. The bowl was made from two clay slabs.

Fig. 210. Transparent glaze, which permits the underglaze design to show through. Underglaze design was brushed on dry greenware with engobes of black, white, dull pink, tan, and brown. Height: 17½ inches. (For construction details, see Chapter 8, page 112.)

Fig. 211. Spraying technique was used to achieve variations of glaze richness and smooth blending of colors. Dark areas were most heavily sprayed, light areas least. Burnt-orange satin-matte glaze. Height: 9½ inches.

Fig. 212. Hanging bells decorated with wax-resist, which was applied to the bisque ware in a free-form pattern. A balance must be achieved between the glazed and unglazed areas. The bells are thrown as cups, turned over, and trimmed. The clay straps are applied as on teapots. The clappers are round disks just slightly smaller than the bells.

Fig. 213. Oxide and glaze combinations on pots from 6 to 12 inches high. *Left to right:* (1) Bisque vase was rubbed with red iron oxide over the design made with a tracing wheel. Top and bottom were dipped into a brown glaze. After the glaze dried, entire pot was sprayed with transparent glaze. (2) Gray glaze was poured over surface of tall bottle, which, after drying, was painted with a dilute solution of vanadium oxide to create the design. Oxide also resulted in an interesting effect by causing the glaze to shrink slightly. (3) Dish was dipped into an opaque white glaze and then overlaid with poured colored glazes for a banding design. When glazes were dry, a design was brushed onto the banded surface with a weak solution of cobalt oxide. (4) Paddled and sgraffito bottle was rubbed with iron oxide on the surface and then waxed before the entire bottle was glazed by pouring over with a tan glaze. Textured appearance was created by sponging on a darker glaze over the first.

8

Combined Forms and Techniques

The techniques of wheel throwing and hand-building and the principles of design and decoration can be used in the construction of larger, more complicated pots than those discussed to this point. The potter who has developed the skill necessary for throwing eight- or ten-inch pots on the wheel may make pots of sixteen or twenty inches, for example, by combining the smaller forms. And the combining of techniques, such as wheel and pinch or wheel and slab, in conjunction with the joining of forms, will permit the potter a variety of pots and pottery creations limited only by his skill and imagination.

This chapter discusses some of the methods of joining forms and combining techniques and provides examples of pots made by these methods. The combinations illustrated are of course not exhaustive and should be regarded only as suggestions.

Experiments in the combining of forms and techniques do not always end in success, even for experienced potters. Don't be upset if your first attempts reveal more enthusiasm and imagination than successful design or technical skill. With time, application, and improvement of technique you will achieve results that will reward you with the feeling of creative accomplishment that comes from having made something that is both technically successful and artistically pleasing.

COMBINING TO MAKE TALL POTS

You can make a pot taller by throwing sections of it separately and joining them together in either the leatherhard or plastic stage. The techniques of joining have been discussed in Chapter 6.

Joining When Leatherhard

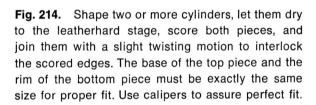

Fig. 214. Shape two or more cylinders, let them dry to the leatherhard stage, score both pieces, and join them with a slight twisting motion to interlock the scored edges. The base of the top piece and the rim of the bottom piece must be exactly the same size for proper fit. Use calipers to assure perfect fit.

Fig. 215. Use small pieces of clay (taken from the cutoff base of the top section and with the same consistency as the clay of the pot). Press the pieces into the seam to help strengthen the seal.

Fig. 216. As the wheel turns moderately slowly, use a loop tool to trim the seal and smooth the surface where the clay was added.

Fig. 217. Work additional clay into the seam if it is needed, and continue filling and trimming until the seam disappears. Finish surface with sponge after trimming.

Joining When Plastic

Clay that is less than leatherhard can be joined and subsequently thrown and shaped further, but it must be of sufficient firmness to permit very cautious handling without distortion. Clay that has set for a half hour to an hour after initial throwing will be about the right consistency for additional work. If more than two pieces are to be used, the bottom ones must be allowed to stiffen before the upper pieces are added.

Fig. 218.   The cylinder thrown first, to be used as the upper half of the pot, sits beside the wheel, rim up. Bottom section, on wheel, is thrown so that the exposed edge can be scored, as shown, and the other section joined to it on the bat. Use calipers to assure perfect fit. Rims to be joined must be left fairly thick; they will be thinned after joining.

Fig. 219.   Turn first cylinder over and score. Note the thickness of rims to be joined.

Fig. 220.   Handle cylinders very carefully. Remember that they are still wet. Spread pressure of your hands over the broadest area possible as you lift clay; set the top cylinder down carefully to avoid collapsing the bottom piece as you position it into place. Work the clay seam together with fingers.

Fig. 221. After making sure that both the inside and outside seams are joined well, turn the wheel slowly to ascertain if the combined cylinders make one straight cylinder. If the cylinder is not straight, collar it to straighten. Then continue throwing the large cylinder to the desired shape. Work slowly to finish a pot of this size.

Fig. 222. Use finishing rubber, flexible rib, or sponge to help shape and finish the pot. Note that the finished pot shows no evidence of the seam.

Fig. 223. Finished, glazed pots made by combining two pieces. Pot on left was decorated by stamping a broad band with a small plastic brush cap and applying wax before the glaze firing. Pot on right was overlaid with several glazes.

MAKING A DOUBLE SPOUT

The wheel and hand methods can be combined to make a cylinder with a double spout.

Fig. 224. After the cylinder is raised and the top portion shaped into fairly straight walls, pinch the top in the middle, reaching far enough down so that the clay does not tear.

Fig. 225. Pinch the clay completely together and then all the way through so that there are two spouts.

Fig. 226. Finish each spout to the shape desired. Since the base cannot be inverted on the wheel and trimmed, it must be trimmed as much as possible before being removed from the wheel.

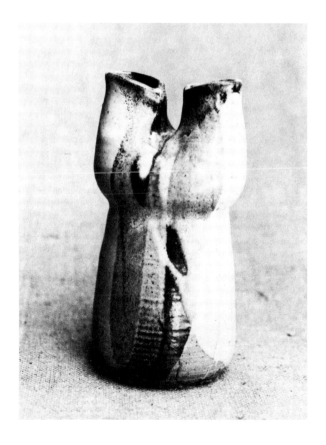

Fig. 227. Finished pot, using glaze overlay. Dark glaze was used to accentuate the split between the spouts.

COMBINING TECHNIQUES

An infinite variety of pottery and sculptured pieces can be made by mixing wheel-thrown pieces and wheel-and-hand combinations. The illustrations that follow give a few ideas for pottery creations of your own.

Wheel Combinations

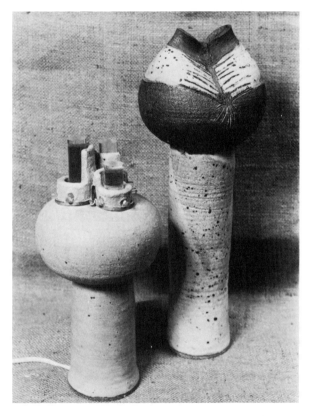

Fig. 229. Hanging planter (5 inches high) made from three pots of the same size, all with rounded bases trimmed when leatherhard and joined at three points by scoring. Heavy, pasty slip was used for extra strength. Pulled handles were attached at points determined with a line guide (see Chapter 5, Fig. 172). Glaze is poured satin matte. (Chain and S hooks, as well as decorative hooks for ceiling mounts, are available at hardware stores.)

Fig. 230. Sculptured weed pots, about 6 inches wide and 3½ inches high, both made by joining two shallow bowls when near leatherhard. Feet on bottom bowls were trimmed before joining. Top bowls were trimmed to low dome shape. After bowls were joined, they were centered on the wheel and the joints trimmed and smoothed. The bowl on the right was paddled into an octagon shape. Wheel-thrown spouts were added last. *Left:* Celadon glaze, with scored rings rubbed with iron oxide and splashed with yellow matte glaze. *Right:* Scored areas were brushed with iron oxides in several colors and then waxed to retain oxide colors and natural clay. Dipped in brown glossy glaze.

Fig. 228. *Left:* Light sculpture, made from wheel-thrown base, center, and three small cylinders of varying heights. Overall height: 11¼ inches. To allow for drying and firing shrinkage, the cylinders, cut chair-shaped, were made with open centers slightly larger than the plexiglass tubes used as lights. All pieces were joined when leatherhard, and small holes punched in the middle section under each of the cylinders to permit light diffusion. Holes for the small plexiglass tubes were cut during leatherhard stage, again slightly larger than the tubes. Hole was cut at base to permit electric cord for socket mounted in bottom section. Decorated with yellow matte glaze and leather thongs. *Right:* Wheel sculpture, made from two wheel-thrown cylinders joined for the base and a spherical form for the top. Height: 16 inches. Sphere was pinched when still wet and carved when leatherhard. All three pieces were joined when leatherhard. Decorated with stony matte glaze, with dark area left in natural clay.

Fig. 231. Multipot hanging sculpture (24 inches high), made from about twenty-five pots thrown at the same time off the mound. Approximately four sizes of pots were used, the larger ones dominant at the middle, the smaller ones at the ends. The pots on each horizontal tier were joined in the leatherhard stage, the pots resting on a cradle of towels and paper to hold them in the desired position. Then all the tiers were joined. The top is pinched together as in Fig. 225. Drying and firing of so complex a piece, with thickness of pots necessarily differing, must be slow. Firing was done in an electric top loading kiln, the sculpture held up with nichrome wire.

Fig. 233. Two-tiered tray, with bowl attached, made in three sections, by Steve O'Loughlin. A mound left in the center of the lower plate was lifted up as a cylinder, to which was attached the separately thrown smaller plate and bowl. Glaze is a combination of three overlaid glazes. Height: 12 inches.

Fig. 232. Multicup candle holder (6½ inches high; 11½ inches in diameter), made from seven cup-shaped, individual candle holders joined together and then attached to a bowl-shaped base. For good design and proportion, the base should be slightly taller than the cups and wide enough to accommodate the base of the center cup and about 1 inch of the surface of each of the other cups. The cups were scored and joined with heavy slip on a board that could be lifted, then covered sandwich fashion with another board, and flipped over. When the board on top was removed, the bottoms of the cups were joined to the base. The construction was dried upside down and bisque fired in the same position to assure against damage because of weight or stress on the joints. Glazing was done by pouring over the entire surface after the base, rims, and areas around the cutout holes were brushed with wax resist.

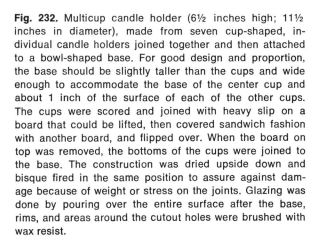

Wheel and Hand Combinations

Fig. 234. Vase and bottle combination shapes, ranging from 5 to 10 inches in height. All are glazed with semimatte glazes and brushed-on oxides. *Left to right:* (1) Wheel-thrown vase with paddled and carved sides and pinched lip. (2) Wheel-thrown round bottle with attached pinched neck. (3) Bottle with wheel-thrown base and pinched top, shaped from a cylinder. Even though the pieces contrast sharply in design, the top section appears to grow naturally from the smooth base. (4) Wheel-thrown bottle with a slab-pinched lid, attached when leatherhard.

Fig. 235. Free-form sculpture with wheel-thrown base. Rolled slabs at left side and middle and snakelike coils were joined to base. Height: 8 inches. Balance of positive and negative space is reinforced by balance of color. Decorated with stony white matte glaze; rubbed with red iron oxide on base and slabs; brown matte coils.

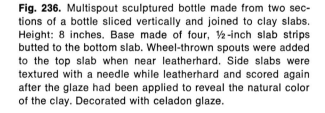

Fig. 236. Multispout sculptured bottle made from two sections of a bottle sliced vertically and joined to clay slabs. Height: 8 inches. Base made of four, ½-inch slab strips butted to the bottom slab. Wheel-thrown spouts were added to the top slab when near leatherhard. Side slabs were textured with a needle while leatherhard and scored again after the glaze had been applied to reveal the natural color of the clay. Decorated with celadon glaze.

Fig. 237. *Left to right:*

Spherical bottle with two spouts. Bottle was initially closed completely and marked for openings the same size as the inside of the spouts, which were joined when all the pieces were near leatherhard. Height: 4½ inches. Decorated by dipping the entire bottle into yellow matte glaze first, then dipping only the top portion into temmoku or dark brown satin-matte glaze.

Triangular three-spouted bottle (height: 7 inches), made by wheel and slab combination. Wheel-thrown cylinder, with slight outward flare, was pinched in at the center from near the base until the lips were an inch apart. At the leatherhard stage a slab cover was joined across the top and holes cut for the wheel-thrown spouts. Decorated with a thin willow green glaze, then overglazed by pouring matte glaze (the dark area) to accentuate the triangular form.

Three-spouted bottle (height: 5¾ inches), made by wheel and pinch combination. Three bottles of slightly different size were thrown and pinched when wet to achieve slumping effect. Additional pinched pieces were added for balance between the bottles and the base, also wheel thrown, slumped, and attached to the bottles when near

leatherhard. Decorated with gray matte glaze, with base dipped into temmoku, which was also poured carefully over the spouts. Finished bottle is black and gray.

Multitiered, three-spouted bottle (height: 13¼ inches), made by wheel and pinch combination. The base, midsection, and center spout were wheel thrown and joined at the leatherhard stage by first attaching a rim of stretched and pinched clay to the top of the base, then adding the midsection and encircling it with the stretched, pinched clay, and finally adding the top section, to which the two other spouts had already been joined. Note the partial spout at the left. Decorated with celadon glaze, which was partially wiped off the pinched areas with a sponge to reveal some of the natural clay.

Tiered, spiraling weed pots (height: 8 inches), made from seven wheel-thrown, spherical pots of diminishing size. When leatherhard, pots were joined at cutaway section of the sides to give greater strength and support flattening during the joining. Smaller pots spiral upward over the large pot to provide physical and visual balance. Decorated with matte glaze.

Fig. 238. *Light sculpture,* 12 inches high and 10 inches in diameter, made from three wheel-thrown pieces (the center is a slightly flared cylinder, and the top and bottom are variations on the bowl shape) joined to each other and to slab strips when leatherhard. (For construction of the clay rings and plexiglass lights, see Chapter 6, Fig. 175.) Satin matte glaze with flowing effect achieved by brushing on temmoku.

Other Examples

Combinations of techniques may also be seen in several pots in previous chapters of the book. A discussion of them will provide further suggestions and ideas for design, decoration, and construction techniques.

Chapter 7, Fig. 176. The doughnut-ring sculpture was thrown on the wheel in three pieces. Height: 10 inches. The ring was made from a doughnut-shaped mass of clay centered on the wheel and opened with the thumb so that the sides, about ¼ inch thick, could be raised on the inside and outside to make a U-shaped trough. The sides of the trough were then gently joined and the seam smoothed with two rubber or flexible ribs, making a fully enclosed doughnut shape. Wheel-thrown base and spout were joined when near leatherhard, with holes punched through the ring above the base and beneath the spout to permit escape of air during drying and firing. Decorated with brown matte, willow green matte, and celadon glaze.

Chapter 7, Fig. 189. The tall cylindrical vases were both made in sections, the smaller one (slightly over 1 foot high) from two cylinders, the taller one (nearly 28 inches high) from three cylinders. All the cylinders were joined during the leatherhard stage, the points of juncture emphasized as features of the design. The base of the taller vase was turned upside down before joining. Note the flared foot, which was the lip of the cylinder when it was thrown.

Chapter 7, Fig. 210. The vase, subtly suggestive of a musical motif, was made using the technique described for the slab planter box. The front and back slabs of the base, traced using templates, were joined to the end, bottom, and top slabs in the near leatherhard stage. The neck was constructed from three small cylinders that were joined and trimmed on the wheel before being attached to the body of the pot. The hollow handles were shaped from slabs and also attached to the body and neck when leatherhard. Remember that in constructions in which hollow forms are attached to other surfaces, holes must be provided to allow air to escape during drying and firing.

9

Firing and Kilns

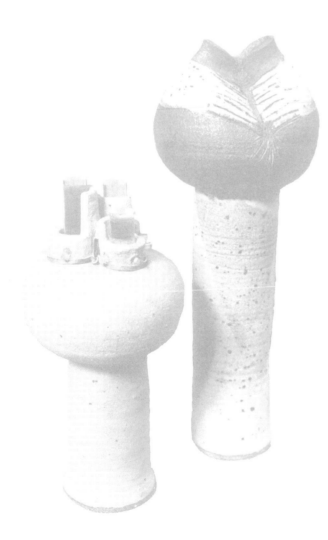

All the preliminary processes and techniques—wedging, throwing, hand-building, decorating, drying—receive their final test in the intense heat of the kiln, which ultimately transforms the clay to stone, the glaze to glass, and the pot to a ceramic creation. Now it is truly "fired earth." To the potter the final glaze firing represents the moment of glory—his moment of truth as an artist and craftsman in clay.

But the firing processes bring not only moments of glory; they can bring disappointment as well. The heat reveals any imperfections and carelessness in the making of the pot. During the bisque firing, clay that has been improperly wedged, with air pockets left in, will break—even explode—with danger to other pots in the kiln. Similarly, water remaining in the clay because of inadequate drying will turn to steam and rupture the pot in trying to escape. Walls that are too thick may crack; walls that are too thin may warp or crack. During the glaze firing, glaze that is too thick may crawl or run, and the glaze will crack, craze, or even break off the pot if it is not appropriate to the clay on which it has been placed.

Potters talk of "happy accidents" that take place in the kiln—unforeseen changes that result in pleasantly unexpected effects. Since accidents may be equally unhappy, however, the ideal firing is one in which the anticipated results are finally realized. The control necessary for such firings is possible even for the reasonably inexperienced potter operating his own kiln if he is attentive to the essentials of firing. This chapter will deal with those essentials—the types of firing, the types of kilns, the operation of the kiln—to guide the potter who does his own firing and, for the potter whose pots are fired by someone else, to explain what the firing processes involve.

BISQUE AND GLAZE FIRINGS

Pots are normally subjected to two firings. The first, the *bisque firing* (also called *biscuit firing*), removes from the clay the chemical water left after air drying and prepares the clay to receive glazes and slips during the decoration. Since unfired clay will absorb water, the purpose of the bisque firing is to transform the clay into a porous, bricklike substance that can absorb the water in the glazes and the slips without turning soft and possibly breaking. Bisque firing is usually done at temperatures of about 1600 degrees F. to 1850 degrees F. for earthenware and stoneware clays. The second and final firing, the *glaze firing* (also called the *gloss firing*), is at a higher temperature in order to bring the clay to maturity and fuse the glaze ingredients to each other and to the clay. For earthenware this temperature is about 2000 degrees F., for stoneware about 2300 degrees F. Porcelain is sometimes fired to a high temperature in the bisque firing (cone 10 to 14) and then fired at a lower temperature for the glaze. If a low-fire glaze is to be put on a stoneware pot, the bisque stoneware can be fired to its maturity, then glazed and fired at the low-fire glaze temperature.

PYROMETRIC CONES

Firing temperatures are only one measure of kiln performance, however, since the duration and extent of firings are determined not by the temperatures alone but by the combined effect of time and temperature on the pots being fired. This effect is recorded by commercially available pyrometric cones placed within the kiln and designed to bend according to the effect of the heat intensity over time in the kiln.

These slender, pyramid-shaped cones are made of materials similar to the bisque ware or glazes being

fired. Thus they provide an accurate gauge of the effect of heat over time on the pots inside the kiln. Normally, three of the cones, mounted on a plaque or base at angles of eight to ten degrees from the vertical, are placed within the kiln in a position where the effect of heat on them may be observed through the peephole in the kiln. The cones are mounted in fixed order on a pad made from a thin coil of clay, with a flattened end for the lead cone to bend into without touching the kiln shelf. The numbers on the cones must face down. The cone that will deform at the lowest temperature is the *guide* or *warning cone;* it is placed at one end of the plaque so that it will bend without touching another cone. The middle cone is the *firing cone,* which will deform at the temperature desired for the particular firing. The third cone is the *guard cone;* if the firing goes beyond the desired point, this cone will deform, with possibly disastrous results to the contents of the kiln. The three cones thus let the potter know when the desired effect of the heat is approaching, when it has arrived (at which point the kiln should be turned off), and when the kiln has been overfired. A fourth cone is often used in a reduction firing to signal the time for reduction.

The numbers used on pyrometric cones are standardized but confusing, for some of the cones de-

Fig. 239. Cone pads for different types of firings. *Left front:* Dark cones are for bisque firing: 010, 09, and 08, for firing at cone 09. *Center:* Light cones are for high fire: 9, 10, and 11, for firing at cone 10. *Rear:* Four cones are used for reduction firing without a pyrometer, the first cone to melt signaling the time for reduction. *Right front:* Pad shows cones after firing to a "soft" cone 10. The firing cone is at about the two o'clock position, instead of a "flat" or "hard" cone 10. Cones 8 and 9 are down, cone 11 starting to bend.

forming at the highest temperatures have numbers that are lower than those deforming at lower temperatures. The following chart gives the standard cone numbers and their temperature equivalents when heated at the rate of 270 degrees F. per hour in an air or oxidizing atmosphere:

Cone Number	Temperature Equivalent[1]	Approximate Color of Kiln Interior[2]	Type of Ware and Glazes[3]
15	2608° F.		
14	2491		
13	2455		
12	2419		
11	2399	White	Porcelain
10	2381		
9	2336		China Bodies
8	2305		Stoneware
7	2264		Salt Glazes
6	2232		
5	2185		
4	2167		China Glaze
3	2134		
2	2124		Semi-vitreous Ware
1	2109		
01	2079		Earthenware
02	2048	Yellow	
03	2014		
04	1940		Low Fire Earthenware
05	1915		Lead Glazes and
06	1830		Low Fire Fritted Glazes
07	1803		
08	1751	Orange	
09	1693		
010	1641		
011	1641		
012	1623		Luster Glazes
013	1566	Cherry	
014	1540	Red	
015	1479		Chrome Red Glazes
016	1458		
017	1377		Overglaze colors,
018	1323		Enamels and
019	1261		Gold
020	1175	Dull Red	
021	1137		
022	1112		

(Courtesy, Edward Orton Jr. Ceramic Foundation, Columbus, Ohio.)

1. The temperature equivalents in this table apply only to Large (2½") Orton Pyrometric Cones when heated at the rate of 270° F. per hour in an air atmosphere.
2. When looking into the peephole all objects that are near the same temperature will be nearly the same color, thus hard to see. Brighter appearing objects are hotter than darker objects. Experience will help one see cones more easily in an evenly heated kiln. Another aid is to set the kiln load so that there is a clear view of elements on the far wall behind the cones.
3. This table is for general information. Consult the manufacturer's instructions for the correct cone number to use and other details. A reliable manufacturer tests his product thoroughly and will be best able to tell how it should be used.

If a firing temperature of 1915 degrees F. is desired, for example, the firing cone would be 05. The warning cone would be one number less—06—and the guard cone one number higher—04.

Commercially available clays and glazes indicate at what cone or cone range they should be fired. It is thus necessary for the potter to coordinate the clay and glazes he uses with the kiln in which the pottery will be fired.

TYPES OF KILNS

An exhaustive discussion of types of kilns is beyond the scope of this book, but it is appropriate—if only to suggest the types of questions that must be answered in the selection of a kiln for personal use—to discuss sizes, types of heat source, and the kinds of firing that can be done with different kilns.

The size of the kiln depends upon several factors: the amount of work to be fired, the facilities available for housing the kiln, and the amount of money the potter wishes to spend. With respect to the last point, it is important not to economize unduly in the purchase of the kiln, for a cheap kiln will likely perform poorly and wear out quickly.

Kilns are available in a wide range of sizes, from small table model kilns with firing chambers of less than one cubic foot to huge kilns for industrial or commercial use. For the home potter a kiln of from four to eight cubic feet is desirable, with a six or seven cubic foot kiln a good average size. To help visualize your needs, stack some empty boxes to fill an area that seems adequate and measure the cubic footage (height times width times depth).

The two heat sources normally used are electricity and gas (natural or propane). Electric kilns have the advantage of cleanliness and convenience of operation, for they do not need to be vented, and their temperature ranges are capable of accommodating all firing needs. Low-fire electric kilns (which range up to about 2000 degrees F.) are capable of firing low-fire earthenware; high-fire electric kilns—either to 2300 degrees F. (cone 8) or 2419 degrees F. (cone 12)—will fire stoneware and even porcelain. Since the upper range of high-fire electric kilns is near the necessary firing temperatures for stoneware and porcelain, however, frequent firings at maximum capacity will, of course, more quickly burn out the heating elements and deteriorate the fire bricks. The most economical use of a kiln is to fire it somewhat below its top capacity.

Gas kilns are of two basic types, updraft and downdraft. An updraft kiln has the burners on the sides or bottom, with the heat rising through the firing chamber, then back down through the center of the kiln, and finally out a chimney at the rear floor. In downdraft gas kilns the chimney serves the same purpose as in a fireplace—to induce a draft—and chimneys vary in size according to the kiln size.

Each potter has his idea of the perfect kiln. But either type—updraft or downdraft—if well designed will serve well. For the potter planning to build a kiln, however, the advantages of a downdraft kiln may be greater because of the relative ease in making adjustments to correct firing deficiencies. It is our experience that firing problems in a poorly designed updraft kiln are more difficult to correct than those in a poorly designed downdraft kiln.

Gas kilns lack some of the convenience of electric kilns but, depending on geographical location, can be more economical to operate and in general require fewer repairs than electric kilns, since there are no elements to burn out. Gas kilns are, on the whole, more versatile than electric kilns: both permit oxidation firing; however, only the former permits reduction firing, which cannot be accomplished in electric kilns without eventually burning out the heating elements. These two types of firings will be discussed next.

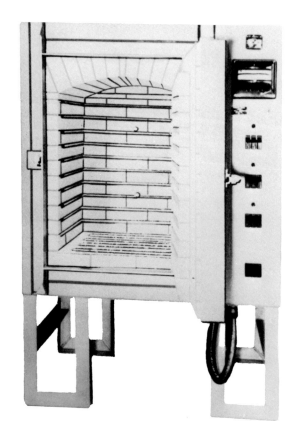

Fig. 240. Paragon top-loading electric kiln, Model A-99B, with a firing capacity of 7 cubic feet. Inside depth: 27 inches; diameter: 23⅜ inches. Middle section may be removed for firing smaller pieces, or 4½ inches blank collar may be added to give inside depth of 31½ inches. Fires to cone 6. Stainless steel or hammertone brown. (*Courtesy Paragon Industries, Inc., Dallas, Tex.*)

Fig. 241. Alpine front-loading electric kiln, Model EF-8, with a firing capacity of 8 cubic feet. Inside height: 29 inches; width: 23 inches; depth: 21 inches. Can be made to operate on 208, 220, or 240 volts, single or three phase. Fires to cone 10 in seven to eight hours. Comes equipped with complete floor shelf, set of supporting posts, and peephole plugs. (*Courtesy, A. D. Alpine, Inc., El Segundo, Calif.*)

Fig. 242. Westwood front-loading gas kiln, Model WCS 106, with a firing capacity of 6 cubic feet. Inside height: 24 inches; width: 24 inches; depth: 18 inches. Fires to cone 10 in six to eight hours and cone 06 in four hours. Designed specifically for the semiprofessional potter. (*Courtesy, Westwood Ceramic Supply Company, City of Industry, Calif.*)

OXIDATION AND REDUCTION FIRINGS

The two principal types of firings are classified as oxidation firing and reduction firing, and both depend upon the atmosphere within the kiln during

the firing. In an oxidation firing, there is sufficient air in the kiln to provide the necessary oxygen. Most firings are accomplished with oxidation, but reduction firing is used for special effects. The reduction is accomplished by reducing the air supply in the kiln so that the gas cannot burn completely. The free carbon that is released in the kiln atmosphere will, at the high temperature of the kiln, combine with the oxygen in the chemical oxides and pull the oxidizable elements (the impurities) from the body of the clay to the surface, where they will react chemically with the glaze. The results of oxidation and reduction firings are radically different, even when the same clay and glazes are used. Copper, which oxidizes green, becomes a deep red in reduction firing. Rutile (tan in oxidation) may become blue; iron in a celadon formula becomes gray green. Glazes generally become more muted and warmer in color than in oxidation firing at the same temperature, and clays become darker and richer.

Reduction firings vary from kiln to kiln and from firing to firing, for no two kilns or firings are exactly alike. A reduction firing is normally done, however, at cones 8 to 10, with the air closed off (by means of a damper or bricks) at red heat (about 1600 degrees F.) and again at cone 9 (2336 degrees F.), with a slight reduction between the two heavier reduction periods. Each of the heavy reduction periods should last from thirty minutes to an hour. The reduction must be done in periods, for the heating of the kiln will not progress (as it must, of course, for the full firing cycle) during a heavy reduction. It may, in fact, even drop. Some potters run a half-hour reduction every hour from red heat to cone 10. Others will run only one reduction for about an hour at cone 9, but with a continual partial reduction all the way from red heat, below which reduction is not possible.

Each potter must find which reduction cycle works best with his kiln and his pots. It is necessary, at least until the best cycle has been established, to keep exact records of each reduction firing.

Reduction firings are not limited to gas kilns, but such firings in electric kilns burn out the heating elements more rapidly than do oxidation firings, since the free carbon combines with these elements as well as with the impurities in the clay and the oxides. A reduction firing is accomplished in an electric kiln by placing mothballs in the peephole. The technique is not advised, however, except under the supervision of an experienced potter.

CHOOSING A KILN

The preceding discussion suggests some of the variables that must be considered in choosing a kiln for one's own use: the size needed, the types of heat source, and the types of firing to be done. Other variables involve economics and, to some degree, geography. In areas where natural gas is not available and propane gas is costly, electric kilns become almost a necessity. On the other hand, the home potter may not be willing to go to the expense of adding the 220-volt hook-up necessary for the larger electric kilns or of extending an existing 220-volt line to the location where the kiln is to be used. Adaptors, incidentally, are available to permit the kiln to be plugged into an electric dryer outlet, but should not be used unless the required amperage for the kiln can be accommodated by the circuit. Electric kilns and gas kilns of the same size are not appreciably different in cost. The determining factors in choice, then, are ultimately the availability of the heat source, the cost of the installation and upkeep, and the types of firing desired. If reduction firings are wanted, a gas kiln is advised. If only oxidation firings are wanted, an electric kiln will serve well. Whatever type of kiln is chosen, it is important to check that the fire bricks in the kiln are adequate. Bricks are classified by the average heat they can take. For example, a K-20 brick will fire to 2000 degrees F., a K-23 brick to 2300 degrees F.

KILN LOADING

After greenware has dried completely, it is ready for stacking in the kiln. Pots to be bisque fired may be stacked upon and inside each other to make maximum use of the space available. Heavier pieces should go on the bottom of the kiln, with lighter pieces on top, and flat pieces should be placed flat to avoid warping. About half an inch of open space should be left between the walls of the kiln and the pieces to be fired to allow for heat movement and, in an electric kiln, to avoid damage to the heating elements. The use of shelves and supports made of refractory materials will allow you to set up several layers of pots. Pots should be placed so that the weight on the shelves is distributed evenly to prevent them from warping. Posts may be placed in either of two arrangements. In smaller kilns, posts can be placed under each corner of the shelf. In larger kilns, however, it is best to use three posts per shelf, two posts on one side (at the corners) and one post on the other side (in the middle of the shelf). If shelves are to be set up side by side, the corner posts can serve for both shelves. This triangular method minimizes the swaying of the shelves and reduces the number of posts needed. Fig. 243 shows four-corner placement in a small kiln, Fig. 244 a roughly triangular post placement in a somewhat larger kiln, Fig. 245 the outside post placement in a large kiln. Posts for successive levels of shelves should always be placed atop each other, as in Fig. 245. Sufficient kiln furniture (shelves, supports, stilts for supporting ware that is glazed all over and cannot be allowed to touch the shelf) to accommodate all types of loads should be purchased at the same time as the kiln. It is advisable to fill the kiln as completely as possible for each firing to make the most economical use of the heat and to distribute the heat evenly in the firing chamber.

Fewer pots can be stacked for a glaze firing, for glazed pots must not be closer than one-eighth of an inch to one another. Glazes that touch will fuse—to each other, to the kiln bottom, and to the kiln shelves. In order to avoid this problem the top surfaces of the shelves should be treated with a heavy layer of kiln wash (about three coats of equal parts kaolin and flint); kiln wash is also available in powdered form from suppliers. In this way glaze that drips can be easily removed, and the chipped places on the pots patched.

For both the bisque and glaze firings, set the plaque of pyrometric cones so that they can be seen through the peephole (check this carefully before stacking the kiln all the way up), but at least six inches from the peephole so that the cool air from the hole will not affect their performance.

Fig. 243. Partially disassembled, modular electric kiln showing components and placement of ware for bisque firing. The short fire-brick posts are stacked one atop the other to build up the necessary shelf height. Before the second shelf is placed, posts will be set behind the pitcher and added to the front posts to equal the height of the right rear posts. The cone pad, made of fire brick, has been placed in position opposite the peephole before the first shelf was placed in kiln. Note the shelf behind the kiln, with cutout areas for the hands on the sides to increase ease of placement inside the kiln. Kiln is by Marshall Crafts, Santa Clara, Calif.

Fig. 244. Top-loading electric bisque kiln, partially loaded. Small cups may be stacked rim to rim or bottom to bottom or placed randomly as shown here if care is taken to avoid chipping.

Fig. 245. Tightly stacked gas kiln ready for glaze firing. Note the cone pad at the lower right, to be viewed through peephole (not shown) in the door. Pots are no closer than ⅛ inch. Glazed planters are fired on rims with grog under rims to allow pots to "slide" on the kiln shelves as they shrink during firing so that they will not crack or warp. Hard fire bricks at bottom of door help to seal the door, but also help to create a downdraft as they pull heat toward the bottom of the kiln.

OPERATING A KILN

After the kiln is stacked, the firing is ready to begin. The initial heating of the kiln should be slow, with the kiln door or cover ajar, so that the mechanical water still in the greenware and the water that is chemically part of both the glazes and the clay can escape as steam. Any water vapor left in the kiln atmosphere will cause defects in the glazes. During a bisque firing, the door should be left ajar for three hours or longer, with the kiln at a temperature under 200 degrees to remove all of the moisture. During a glaze firing, the door or cover should be left ajar for about two hours, then closed so that the kiln can be brought to the required temperature.

The firing will take several hours, depending on the efficiency of the kiln, the size of the load, and the top temperature desired. Keeping watchful attention and careful records during the first firings of a kiln will give you an idea of what to expect and will free you during later firings to go about other things as the kiln heats.

When the guide cone deforms, it is necessary to keep a careful eye on the firing cone, for the temperature rise necessary for deforming the firing cone will not be very great. When the firing cone is bent over more than half way, but before the tip has dipped level with the top of the plaque, the kiln should be turned off. Then seal it tightly and leave it to cool naturally. The cooling should take about one and a half times longer than the firing. An overnight wait is advised. The door of the hot kiln should under no circumstances be opened, for the resulting extreme change of temperature will crack the pots and possibly explode them.

When the kiln is completely cool it can be unloaded. If the pots have been removed before they are completely cool, they will make tinkling sounds for some time as they cool, and some glazes may shiver if the pots cool too rapidly. It is best not to unload the kiln until it has cooled sufficiently so that the pots can be handled comfortably without asbestos gloves.

Commercial kilns come with instructions for their use and maintenance. For safety and best performance, these instructions should be read carefully and attentively followed.

FIRING AND GLAZING PROBLEMS

Problems involved in firing can result in defects in the glazes. Firing too quickly, for instance, will cause granular and bubble defects in the glazes. Most defects that appear in the glazes, however, are the result of faulty preparation of the clay, improper glazing, or the use of glaze inappropriate to the clay. In the last case, the glaze and clay will contract at different rates during the cooling. If the difference is great enough, the pot will be ruined. The common glaze flaws of *crazing, shivering, crawling,* and *pinholing* are defined and their causes discussed in detail in the following chapter.

FIRING SAFETY PRECAUTIONS

A properly placed and ventilated commercial kiln or well-made custom kiln presents almost no danger from the standpoint of fire; to cause fire damage to an enclosing or adjacent structure a kiln would have to collapse during a firing—a highly unlikely prospect. Nevertheless, the intense heat generated by a kiln demands respect, and proper precautions must be taken.

Even with thick insulating bricks, the outside of kilns become very hot. Flammable materials should never be placed near kilns, and children should not be permitted in the kiln area. It makes sense to keep a fire extinguisher (of the ABC type) near the kiln.

When removing the plug from the peephole to check the temperature, always wear asbestos gloves. Asbestos gloves should also be worn when handling kiln furniture, which usually remains hot longer than pots. Never place your face closer than two feet from the peephole, since the heat can sear face and eyes. Wearing dark glasses will shield the eyes and will help you to see the hot cones more clearly.

A gas kiln presents special ventilation problems. It should be in a well-ventilated location, either outdoors or in a specially ventilated room. If indoors, it should be equipped with an air intake, a hood flue, and possibly an exhaust fan. Local fire codes should be checked regarding indoor gas kilns.

When lighting a gas kiln, have the flame near the gas orifice before turning on the gas. If the flame is blown out, allow plenty of time for the accumulated gas to dissipate before attempting to relight. For emergency shutoff, it is wise to have a main shutoff valve some distance from the burners.

Use lots of common sense!

10

Basic Glaze Formulation

The formulation of glazes may appear an overwhelming undertaking to the beginner, one that requires a sophisticated background in chemistry and physics even to get started. Unfortunately, many potters have inadvertently perpetuated this notion with tales of disastrous kiln experiences and bad glaze batches. However, there are logical and straightforward methods for becoming acquainted with glaze formulation that need not frighten off anyone. In this chapter we will discuss the properties and proportions of ingredients in a base glaze, show how to modify the base glaze, discuss glaze colorants, and outline procedures for experimenting with and testing colorants. After following these procedures, you may wish to consult some of the excellent books on glazes, such as Daniel Rhodes's *Clay and Glazes for the Potter* and David Green's *Pottery Glazes;* John Conrad's *Ceramic Formulas: The Complete Compendium;* and the glaze formulations by Richard Behrens featured in *Ceramics Monthly.*

A BASE GLAZE

By and large, the materials used in a base glaze are the most common ingredients in the earth's crust: feldspars, which contain alumina and silica; silica, called flint or quartz in some formulas; whiting, pure calcium carbonate, which contributes calcium oxide to a glaze; and kaolin, generally a pure white primary type of clay. There are usually overlappings of the elements that the ingredients bring into the glaze; for example, silica is a component of feldspar, but silica can also be added separately.

The basic formula we shall discuss will fire to about cone 8 and has four ingredients:

Feldspar	40%
Silica	30
Whiting	20
Kaolin	10
	100%

Feldspar is an ideal glaze material for the stoneware temperature range, for, depending on the variety of spar used, it melts with no additions between cones 4 and 12 to a stiff, opaque glass. Because of this valuable characteristic, most stoneware glazes contain between 30 and 60 percent feldspar. Since feldspar has a high alkaline quality, however, too much of it in a glaze may make the glaze craze—that is, develop a fine network of surface cracks. This tendency must be corrected by a reduction of the feldspar in favor of either silica or clay.

A proportion of 30 percent silica should be enough to insure a smooth, hard glaze without defects such as crazing or crackling. Silica, commonly called quartz or flint by potters, comes from various kinds of flint rock and is gray, brown, or black in its natural state. This material is refined as a white powder called silica flour or potter's flint. Most stoneware glazes contain between 15 and 40 percent flint, although some glazes do not contain silica as a separate ingredient. All of them, however, contain silica as part of their composition.

Silica is the major and sometimes the only glass-forming material present in a glaze. Theoretically, silica alone could be used to form a glaze if sufficient heat were available and an adequate refractory (heat resistant) clay body could be found to apply it to. In practice, however, silica is combined with other materials called *fluxes*, which lower its melting point to a more practical temperature range. Silica has the valuable property of readily combining with such fluxing agents as sodium, potassium, lead, calcium, and boron to form glasses of varying viscosity and melting temperature.

In our base glaze, sodium, potassium, and calcium are present as fluxes in adequate amounts to cause the silica to form a glass at around 2300 degrees F. If we were to add increasing amounts of flint to the glaze, the melting temperature would increase accordingly. If we were to increase the flint and maintain the firing temperature of 2300 degrees F., a dulling of the gloss would occur until, with increasing amounts of flint, a point would be reached when a smooth glass would no longer form. The glaze would in essence be *underfired*. Beyond a certain point the glaze defect called shivering (the breaking away of the glaze from the pot) would occur. If we were to subtract amounts of flint from the glaze, the glass would become shinier and more fluid, as well as softer, and subject to the defect of crazing, which is the opposite of shivering.

The third material, whiting, is pure calcium carbonate and is derived by milling and purifying limestone rock. It has a melting temperature of 2572 degrees F. but acts as a flux in glazes. It is an important and valuable glaze material, for it imparts hardness to the glaze, serves as a flux over wide temperature ranges, and is available cheaply almost everywhere. Most glazes contain calcium. In low temperature lead and alkaline glazes, calcium contributes hardness and creates a less soluble glaze. Increasing the amount of calcium oxide in a glaze may cause a dulling of the surface without affecting transparency. Further additions of whiting will make the glaze surface more and more matte. Care should be taken always to use the same brand of whiting, for the material will vary from one manufacturer to another in particle size and purity.

Several other materials besides whiting contain calcium carbonate. Among them are dolomite, colemanite, and bone ash or calcium phosphate. These materials should be tried as substitutes for the whiting in this base glaze formula. A good procedure is to replace whiting with another material in increments of 5 percent until, in the final batch, the whiting has been totally replaced. For example, see table on page 123.)

Replacing one material with another in this manner may yield many interesting and beautiful effects. Don't let your spirits droop, however, if your expectations prove greater than the results achieved.

The final ingredient in the base glaze is kaolin, a pure clay substance. It is the most valuable of the clays because its freedom from iron oxides allows it to burn to a white color. It is used extensively by commercial china manufacturers in the production of white ware and is the most common clay used in the production of glazes for all temperature ranges.

Glaze A		Glaze B		Glaze C		Glaze D	
Feldspar	40%	Feldspar	40%	Feldspar	40%	Feldspar	40%
Flint	30	Flint	30	Flint	30	Flint	30
Whiting	15	Whiting	10	Whiting	5	Dolomite	20
Dolomite	5	Dolomite	10	Dolomite	15	Kaolin	10
Kaolin	10	Kaolin	10	Kaolin	10		100%
	100%		100%		100%		

Kaolin performs several important functions in a glaze. Besides introducing alumina and silica, it helps to keep the other glaze materials in suspension when they are mixed with water. When the glaze is applied to a pot, kaolin helps to form a tough coating that resists abrasion and allows the raw glazed ware to be handled more easily without damage to the glaze coating. Because of its refractory nature—it melts at cones 32 to 34—kaolin combines slowly in the glaze melt and keeps the glaze from flowing off the vertical walls of a pot. The presence of alumina introduced by kaolin retards crystallization of the glaze, therefore maintaining a clear glass with a smooth surface. If too much kaolin is introduced, however, the glaze becomes more opaque and matte, and if a very large amount is added (i.e., 25 to 50 percent), the glaze no longer forms a smooth glass at the intended firing temperature but rather gives a rough, dry, or underfired appearance.

A good experiment to try with this base glaze is to increase the kaolin content by adding 5 percent more of that ingredient *after* the batch has been mixed. For example:

Feldspar	40%
Silica	30
Whiting	20
Kaolin	10
	100
+ Kaolin	5
	105%

With this method, the total percentage increases by 5 percent with each increment. Another 5 percent increment of kaolin will thus give 20 percent kaolin in a total percentage of 110. If a formula totaling 100 is desired, each constituent of the glaze is divided by the sum total of materials used. For example:

Feldspar	$40 \div 110 =$	.3636 $=$	36.36%
Flint	$30 \div 110 =$	.2727 $=$	27.27
Whiting	$20 \div 110 =$	.1818 $=$	18.18
Kaolin	$20 \div 110 =$	.1818 $=$	18.18
	110	.9999 $=$	99.99%

This computation may be set up as a ratio, as follows:

$$\frac{\% \text{ of ingredient}}{\text{Total } \% \text{ of ingredients}} = \frac{X}{100}$$

For the kaolin in the above example, therefore, the ratio would be:

$$\frac{20}{110} = \frac{X}{100}$$

$$110X = 2000$$

$$X = \frac{2000}{110} = \frac{200}{11} = 18.18$$

In general, it is best to compute ingredient additions on the basis of 100 percent, for subsequent additions of oxides for colorants can be made more accurately this way.

Another useful experiment is to replace the kaolin in the glaze with another type of clay, such as fire clay, ball clay, earthenware, or even a clay found in your backyard. Since the impurities brought in by these clays cause them—and hence the glaze—to fuse at lower temperatures, caution should be exercised in this test. Placing a pad of fired clay under the test pot will insure against an overly fluid glaze that runs on to the kiln shelf, causing a disagreeable mess.

OTHER SIMPLE BASE GLAZES

Several simple glazes can be made with 50 percent colemanite (also known as Gertsley borate) and 50 percent of another substance. Half colemanite and half plastic vitrox (P. V.) clay works well at almost all stoneware temperatures (cones 5 to 10). The P. V. clay is like a potash feldspar. The slight solubility of the colemanite will cause the glaze to deflocculate (that is, to gather into clumps or "flocks"), and, because of this tendency, the glaze will appear thicker after it has been allowed to stand for some time. The addition of 15 percent Zircopax to this glaze creates an opaque, almost opalescent white that is an excellent liner for food containers.

A mixture of 50 percent colemanite and 50 percent nepheline syenite clay is a good glaze for lower temperatures, particularly for Raku. Again, 10 or 15 percent Zircopax can be added as an opacifier.

Colemanite is often used as a low temperature flux because of the presence of boron, which melts at fairly low temperatures. Zircopax can be added to any clear glaze to make it an opaque white.

Albany slip clay, with its high iron content, fluxes at such a low temperature (cone 8, 2300 degrees F.) that it can be used by itself as a glaze. This is the brown glaze found on old bean crocks and whiskey jugs in antique shops.

COLOR AND TEXTURE

Up to this point we have discussed only the materials used to form a base or clear, colorless glaze, and have suggested how the melting temperature, surface reflectance, and clarity can be adjusted. Most glazes, however, have color and texture, which can be achieved in several ways.

Glazes may be colored or textured by impurities present in the materials that constitute the base glaze. For example, if a fire clay is used to introduce alumina into the glaze, some impurities such as iron or rutile may also be introduced, coloring the glaze tan or light green. The celadon glaze used by the Chinese is green because of small amounts of iron introduced either as impurities in the glaze or in the clay body to which the glaze is applied.

The more usual method of altering the color or texture of a glaze is by the direct addition of metallic coloring oxides or prepared glaze stains. The most commonly used coloring oxides are iron, copper, cobalt, rutile, manganese, nickel, and chromium.

The chemical names and formulas for these oxides are:

$CoCo_3$	Cobalt Carbonate
CoO	Cobalt Oxide
Co_2O_3	Cobalt Oxide
CuO	Copper Oxide
$CuCO_3$	Copper Carbonate
Cr_2O_3	Chromium Oxide
FeO	Ferrous Oxide
Fe_2O_3	Iron Oxide (Hematite)
Fe_3O_4	Iron Oxide (Magnetite)
MnO	Manganese Oxide (Manganosite)
$MnCO_3$	Manganese Carbonate
NiO	Nickel Oxide
Ni_2O_3	Nickel Peroxide
TiO_2	Titanium Oxide (Rutile)
V_2O_5	Vanadium Oxide

Following is a table that shows the effect of various metallic coloring oxides in a base glaze on both oxidation and reduction. Effects may vary with the base glaze used.

		Oxidation		Reduction
Material	%	Result	%	Result
Iron oxide, red	.5 – 5.	Straw to tan.	.5 – 1.5	Light gray or green to blue green. Celadon.
	5. –15.	Tan to dark brown to black, increasingly darker as more iron is added.	1.5 – 3.	Blue green to olive to dark olive green.
			3. – 5.	Dark olive to brown to rust.
			5. –10.	Rust to temmoku to saturated iron red.
			10. –15.	Iron red to dark iron red to plum. High concentrations of iron may create dull, muddy glazes. In a proper base glaze high in silica, however, spectacular effects may result.

| | Oxidation | | Reduction | |
Material	%	Result	%	Result
Copper carbonate	.5 – 2. 2. – 4. 4. – 8.	Light green to blue green. Blue green to turquoise. Turquoise to ultramarine to metallic green to black.	.25– .5 .5 – 1. 1. – 3.	Copper red (must contain between .5 and 1% tin oxide for color to develop). Copper red to dark copper red. Dark copper to metallic black.
Cobalt carbonate. (Black cobalt oxide is approximately twice as strong in tinting strength as cobalt carbonate.)	.25– .5 .5 – 1.5 1.5 – 3. 3. – 5.	Pale blue to light blue. Light to medium blue. Medium to dark blue. Dark blue to black. (Large percentages of cobalt may flux the glaze and cause it to flow excessively.)		Approximately the same as oxidation with the exception that iron in the clay body has a greater effect on a reduction glaze, causing a softening or muting of the color.
Rutile (ceramic grade)	5. –10.	Tan to textured light brown. (Rutile is used more as a color modifier and texturing agent than as a coloring oxide.)	3. –10.	Textured tan to cream matte to crystalline brown. With iron, yellows may result. With 5–10% colemanite, beautiful blues and purples may be had, and .5% cobalt may yield greens.
Manganese carbonate. (Black manganese is twice as powerful and may yield spots because it is coarser.)	4. 6.	Medium purple. Dark purple. (Do not use with chromium oxide, as muddy colors result.)	4.	Brown. Manganese is a very weak colorant in reduction, but if used with a small percent of cobalt may give interesting blues. With rutile, an interesting mottled brown results.
Nickel oxide	2. – 5.	Gray to brown usually, but may produce blues and greens in the presence of zinc or magnesia. Another "color modifier."	1. – 3.	Gray or gray brown.
Chromium oxide	.5 – 2.	Light to dark green. Pinks may be produced by adding up to 3% tin oxide. Zinc will produce browns. Chrome has a tendency to "migrate" to adjacent glazed pots while firing. If such a neighboring glaze contains tin oxide, pink patches may develop.	.5 – 1.	Approximately the same results as in oxidation. Usually not as good in reduction firing.

Matte and mottled textures may also be achieved through the direct addition of metallic oxides. Matte textures can be made through the addition of rutile (5 to 10 percent), titanium dioxide (5 to 10 percent), zinc oxide (to 25 percent), feldspars (to 20 percent), whiting (to 20 percent), and barium (to 15 percent). Mottled effects are made by the addition of rutile, vanadium, and ammonium metavandate.

BASE GLAZES AND COLORANTS

The following base glazes may be modified with coloring agents as indicated to achieve a number of effects. These glazes may be used in oxidation firing, but work best with reduction firing.

Albany Slip Glaze (Cones 7–9) *

Albany Slip	60%
F-4 Feldspar	25
Whiting	10
Colemanite	5
	100%

* Formula courtesy of Thano Johnson.

Dry mix the glaze. Add the mix to water and stir until it has the consistency of heavy cream.

For blue brown, add:	Rutile	5%
	Cobalt Carbonate	.5%
For medium temmoku, add:	Red Iron Oxide	5%
For iron red, add:	Red Iron Oxide	7%

Basic White Matte (Cones 9–10)

F-4 Feldspar	35%
Whiting	8
Talc	8
Kaolin	18
Dolomite	16
Silica	10
Bone Ash	5
	100%

For yellow ochre, add:	Red Iron Oxide	2%
	Rutile	5%
For purple blue, add:	Rutile	3%
	Cobalt Carbonate	.5%

Shaner Base (Cone 10)

Kingman (or Custer) Spar	47%
EPK	20
Whiting	19
Talc	4
Bone Ash	10
	100%

For red, add:	Red Iron Oxide	4%
	Rutile	1%
	Bone Ash (additional)	2%
For yellow, add:	Rutile	4%
	Red Iron Oxide	2%

Transparent Glaze (Cone 9)

Glaze Spar 56	44%
EPK	10
Flint	28
Whiting	18
	100%

LOW TEMPERATURE GLAZES

Glazes that fire below cone 5 are generally referred to as low-fire glazes. The addition of coloring oxides gives these glazes a brilliant and colorful surface, but they normally lack the hardness and durability that are necessary in wares that serve a utilitarian purpose. They usually have a very glassy appearance. Reliable low-fire glazes in a variety of types— bisque, matte, gloss, crackle—are available from several suppliers, among them Amaco, Duncan, Leslie, Secent, and Westwood.

TESTING A GLAZE FOR COLOR

The usual procedure for testing a glaze for color is to mix a quantity, say 1,000 grams, of the base dry glaze. This batch is then sifted through a fine mesh sieve (80 to 100 mesh) two or three times to insure a uniform mixture, then weighed out in 50 or 100 gram batches. Cupcake cups, small Styrofoam cups, or plastic sandwich bags are useful to contain these small batches. Next, a code sheet is prepared so that the glazes can be readily identified. This sheet should include the formula for the base glaze as well as a code identification for each modification. For example:

Base Glaze A		Test Codes	
Feldspar	40	A–"A"	.5% iron
Silica	30	A–"B"	1.0% iron
Whiting	20	A–"C"	2.0% iron
Kaolin	10		
	100	etc.	

The coloring oxides are now weighed out and added to the small batches. Simply write the letter of the corresponding test on the test pot with iron oxide. When the test is fired, the code can be easily read and the result noted for future reference. A great deal of confusion is avoided when test records are kept. Be sure to file the code sheets where you can find them, and note the results of all tests, successful or not. Often, a test that seems disappointing at first can take on greater value at a later time.

MAKING TEST TILES

Test tiles may be made by several methods, but for the most complete testing of the new glaze, tiles should have both horizontal and vertical test surfaces. You may roll out a coil of clay about ¾ inches in diameter and then flatten it with a rolling pin or dowel to ¼ inch thickness. Cut the strips into 3 inch lengths, which should then be bent into an L shape. Or you may throw a shallow, pie shell shape (bowl fashion), ¼ inch thick, cut out the center, and then cut out L-shaped wedges about an inch wide from

the outside ring. In either case, the tiles must be bisque fired before they are used for glaze testing, and the test code written on the back with iron oxide before the glaze test firing. Glaze is applied to both the horizontal and vertical surfaces by brushing, dipping, or pouring. Fig. 246 shows test tiles that have been mounted for easy reference.

Larger test tiles are made by throwing small dish-shaped forms about 3 inches in diameter. These have the advantage of being closer in appearance to an actual pot, and the large surface is easier to examine. The test code is written with iron oxide on the bottom of the test dish. Another method is to use a bisque cylinder on which several glazes have been applied, though the cylinder will not reveal the performance of the glaze on a horizontal surface (see Fig. 246).

Small test tiles may be glued to index cards containing their formulas, results, and comments. The results of any test can then be easily stored and seen at a glance.

Fig. 246. Test tiles mounted on panel. Tiles in top row were fired by reduction, those in bottom row by oxidation. Placing the tiles above and below the tags indicating the oxides and percentages permits easy comparison. Base glaze formula is on card at right. Several glazes have been tested on the bisque cylinders. Note the test codes and arrows done with iron oxide.

TESTING FOR WATER CONTENT

Glaze tests should be of the proper consistency for use in future batches of the glaze. Care should be taken that all tests have proportionately equal amounts of water, so that variations in glaze thickness can be controlled from test to test. An extra 100 grams of glaze should be reserved to use as a test for water content. Small amounts of water should be added to the dry powdered glaze until the glaze mixture has the consistency of coffee cream. This can then be applied to a piece of broken bisque ware to check how thickly the glaze builds up on the ware. If it seems too thick, water should be added drop by drop until the desired consistency is reached. The test batch should be mixed in a graduated beaker, on the outside of which the beginning water level and the final water level can be marked with a grease pencil to insure that all test batches have equal amounts of water. It should be remembered that tests with 10 to 15 percent additions of material will require slightly more water than those containing 0.5 to 5 percent additions.

When the correct amount of water has been ascertained, the rest of the tests can be mixed. The most accurate results occur when the test glazes are carefully and completely mixed. If possible, they should be screened wet through an eighty-mesh sieve. Since this is a time-consuming process, however, an alternate method is to screen each test batch dry several times, then place it and the correct amount of water in a plastic jar with a tightly sealed lid, along with some of the porcelain balls or flint pebbles obtainable from ceramic suppliers. The jar is shaken like a spray paint can. The porcelain balls or flint pebbles help to homogenize the glaze. For best results, some glazes—such as copper red or celadon—should be mixed in a ball mill, a machine for pulverizing and grinding either wet or dry materials.

SUGGESTIONS FOR THE BEGINNING GLAZE CHEMIST

1. Find an inexpensive local source for as many as possible of the glaze materials you use. Special imported chemicals and ones not available locally are expensive to ship and are often hard to get. Check with schools or other potters for sources of supply and for possible local materials to use as substitutes in glaze formulas.

2. Buy materials in the largest quantities you can afford and store. Prices on raw materials decrease dramatically when you buy in bulk.

3. Buy a good gram scale. It is worth the extra cost to buy a tare beam model, for it will allow you to place a large receptacle on the balance table and thus weigh large amounts of materials at one time.

4. Don't try for exotic effects until you know what your materials will do. Stick to the simple, proven formulas you know will work. Test any variations on these thoroughly before you mix a large batch. Don't simply throw in "a little more of this or that." The same goes for unfamiliar glaze formulas. Test them carefully before making up large batches; what has promised to be fire-engine red may turn out to be a dingy brown.

5. Some glazed materials—such as lead, cadmium, barium, and copper—are toxic. Avoid prolonged contact with these, and avoid breathing their dust. Mark them as poisons and store them away from ignorant hands. You should, in fact, avoid breathing the dust from any glaze materials, for it settles in the lungs; extreme overexposure to abrasive dusts can cause silicosis, commonly called "miner's disease" or "black lung." A mask should be worn when large amounts of materials are mixed.

6. Keep glaze chemicals dry. Store them in clearly labeled coffee cans or plastic buckets.

7. Keep good notes on your tests and firing results. Develop a studio library of written material, books, and periodicals, study them carefully, and review them often. Talk to other potters and gather as much practical information as you can—but be sure to *check suggestions out* before you use them.

SPECIAL TYPES OF GLAZES

It will be useful to have some familiarity with special types of glazes and glazing techniques, even if you have no plans to deal with them immediately.

A *luster glaze* is an *overglaze* applied over a regular glaze after it has been fired. The overglaze is painted on the glazed pot, which is then refired at a low temperature to bind the luster to the glaze. Commercial luster glazes are readily available. They fire at approximately cone 018, 1323 degrees F.

Crystalline glazes, which can be used only on porcelain, are something of an abnormality in glazes. Because of their low or absent alumina content, crystals form in these glazes during a special cooling period. The temperature at which crystals begin to form is determined through experiment, and when this temperature is reached during the cooling process, the rate of cooling is drastically reduced. Crystalline glazes are generally fired in a high-fire electric kiln in which the rate of cooling can be accurately controlled. These glazes require considerable sophistication to produce and are not recommended for the beginner.

Salt glazing is a relatively old technique of glazing that was widely used on old German beer steins and on stoneware crocks and jugs during the nineteenth century. Salt glazing requires only one firing. Glazing by hand is not necessary, although unfired pots may be decorated with oxides, engobes, or glaze. The firing progresses to maturity as a normal stoneware firing. At the point the clay reaches maturity, salt is introduced into the kiln through a port in front of the burner. The salt volatilizes, with the sodium from the salt joining with the silica in the clay to create a glaze. Repeated saltings will build up the glaze to the desired thickness. It is necessary, or at least advisable, to have small rings or pieces of clay placed in the kiln so that they can be pulled out during the firing process to check on the thickness of the glaze. Once the glaze is thick enough, the kiln is turned off.

Since the glaze is relatively clear, it will pick up the color of the clay. Heavy iron clay will yield a dark brown glaze; clays with little or no iron will produce tans and grays.

Because the salt accumulates in the kiln and is released from the bricks during each firing, a separate kiln must be used for salt glazing. A downdraft kiln, constructed of hard fire brick, is preferable to contain the salt vapor. A word of caution: hydrochloric acid is formed as the salt vaporizes and escapes as a fog. Thus, salt glazing is best done out of doors, away from people. In a heavily populated area, however, common baking soda (purchased in commercial quantities) will substitute for salt. Like salt (sodium chloride), baking soda (sodium bicarbonate) contains sodium, the element necessary for the salt glazing, and with baking soda there are no harmful by-products.

RAKU

An especially interesting and popular type of firing is the Raku technique, employed by Japanese and Korean potters for hundreds of years in making ceremonial tea bowls. Raku firing clay, a porous stoneware body which contains a high percentage of grog that permits radical changes of temperature without cracking, is commercially available or may be made by mixing 10 to 20 percent of twenty- or thirty-mesh grog into a stoneware body. Most clays with a high grog content will work for Raku. Raku glazes, which are low-fire glazes, are also available from suppliers or may be mixed in the studio. A good glaze is half colemanite and half P. V. clay.

Raku pots are typically small bottles, bowls, or cups; but pottery forms of any type or reasonable size may be Raku fired. After the pots have been bisque fired, they are glazed and decorated with oxides and then dried again near a red-hot kiln or on top of the kiln to remove all moisture from the glaze and to preheat the pots. The kiln is generally a small gas or electric kiln, one with a lid that can be opened easily and quickly during the firing. When the kiln has been heated to 1600 degrees F., the pots are quickly placed into it with long-handled tongs (the potter should wear asbestos gloves) and allowed to fire to the red-hot stage (about 1750 to 2000 degrees F., depending on the glaze). When it can be seen through the peephole that the glaze has fluxed or melted, the pots are removed with tongs and placed in a covered metal bucket or barrel (a twenty-gallon trash container works well) about one-third filled with a combustible substance—straw, sawdust, leaves, confetti, wood shavings—and then immediately covered to provide a reduction atmosphere that will give the glazes unusual and unexpected qualities. The reduction is controlled by the length of time the pots are left in the container.

After a few minutes the pots can be removed (again with tongs) and placed in a container of water. If pots are left in the open air to cool, there will be some reoxidation. Placing them in water prevents the reoxidation and retains all the effects of the reduction.

The results of Raku are rapid, dramatic, and individual. If a good effect is achieved, the identical procedure may be tried again, but it is unlikely that precisely the same result will be attained. This is part of the excitement of Raku firing.

Fig. 247. Small Raku pots, about 3 inches high, variously decorated.

GLAZE FLAWS

Any quality of a glaze that interferes with the intended function or aesthetic of the pot can be considered a glaze flaw. For example, if the glazed surface on the inside of a cup or bowl is rough because of underfiring, the function as well as the appeal of the piece is inhibited. Food can become trapped because of the rough surface, and the pot may be difficult to clean. The way to correct this glaze flaw is simply to fire the pot again to the temperature at which the glaze matures.

Glaze flaws occur for many different reasons, and when one exists it is important to identify it, check its cause or causes, and understand its various remedies. The cause of glaze flaws is not always easy to determine, for they can be caused by an imbalance between the glaze and the clay body, improper application of the raw glaze, overfiring, underfiring, dusty or dirty bisque ware, or poorly crafted ware. The following checklist defines some of the most common glaze flaws, explains why they occur, and suggests how they can be remedied or avoided. As a general rule, you should first give attention to application and firing procedures before attempting to make glaze formula adjustments.

Crazing is a network of fine cracks in the surface of a glaze and is caused by the unequal expansion of the glaze coating relative to the expansion of the clay body. The glaze is under tension and cracks as it attempts to conform to the pot. To correct crazing:

1. Add flint, feldspar, or clay to the raw glaze.

2. Increase boron in favor of flint by adding colemanite or another material rich in boron.

3. Increase the firing temperature.

4. Decrease the glaze content of the high-expansion oxides sodium and potash.

5. Apply a thinner application of the glaze and decrease the rate of cooling.

Shivering is the opposite of crazing. The glaze is under more than normal compression, the result of its contracting more slowly than the clay, and it breaks away from the pot. In severe cases the ware itself will break, a defect called *shattering.* To correct shivering:

1. Decrease the silica content of the glaze with a corresponding increase of flux, soda, potash, or lime.

2. Raise the melting point of the glaze by decreasing boric acid and increasing silica.

3. Cool the kiln more slowly.

Crawling is the beading up of the glaze in segregated areas on the pot surface. To correct crawling:

1. Decrease the clay content, the zinc oxide, the feldspar, or the bone ash in the glaze. Too much of any one of these ingredients causes crawling.

2. Apply a thinner application of the glaze or decrease its viscosity by adding water.

3. Allow the raw glaze to dry somewhat before firing or before coating a second glaze over the first.

4. Make sure the bisque ware is free of dirt and dust before applying glaze.

5. Fire the bisque ware at a higher temperature. Underfired bisque causes the glaze to build up too thickly.

6. Increase the *water-smoking* period of the firing, the early part of the firing when the atmospheric water is driven off as steam.

Pinholing appears in the form of minute holes in the surface of the glaze. To correct pinholing:

1. Make sure the bisque ware is free of dirt and dust before applying glaze.

2. Cool the kiln more slowly.

3. Increase the water-smoking period of the firing.

4. Apply the glaze more thinly, especially viscous matte glazes.

5. Add flux to the glaze to make it more fluid.

6. Reduce the amount of zinc or rutile in the glaze.

7. Give the kiln a "soaking" period at top temperature to allow the glaze to smooth out.

As indicated in these suggestions, glaze flaws are sometimes the result of improper application of the raw glaze. Glazing too thickly causes running, blistering, crawling, pinholing, and crazing. Glazing too thinly can result in rough, uninteresting surfaces not of the expected color. Uneven application of the glaze can result in undesirable streaks or splotches.

Fig. 248. Pot on left illustrates crawling, in this case a "happy accident" because the texture is pleasing and the function of the pot not inhibited by the texture. Normally, a crawl will pull an entire section of glaze off the pot. Blistering, caused by too heavy a glaze application, can be seen on the candle holder at the right.

Fig. 249. The glaze on this pot has run during firing. One glaze was applied over another, the combination of glazes fluxing at a lower temperature than the firing and causing the glazes to run almost completely off the top section of the pot and form a mass at the base.

II

The Business of Pottery

MARKETING POTTERY

For the home and hobby potter who continues to develop in artistic skill and craftsmanship, the time will inevitably come when he is faced with the problem of what to do with the pots he is making. His own home can accommodate only a limited number of bottles, vases, bowls, and sculptured pieces, as well as cooking and tableware, before taking on the appearance of a museum or gallery. And although relations and friends may be delighted to receive pottery as gifts on a few occasions, there is a limit to this, too. Where does the potter go—or, rather, what does the potter do—when supply exceeds demand?

Let's suppose you face this problem. You have found pottery making to be a fulfilling pursuit, and you know both subjectively and objectively that the pottery you produce has merit. It looks good to you, measured alongside other pottery you see; and the people who see it find it attractive enough to want to own.

The commercial world of pottery is but a step away. If your circumstances and inclinations permit, you can become a part of it—building from your home studio a well-equipped pottery workshop.

Elsewhere we have spoken briefly of some of the equipment you need—a wheel, a kiln, tools, and space. If you are seriously interested in pursuing pottery as a part-time or full-time vocation, however, the matter of equipment becomes a major concern. It is wise to proceed slowly in purchasing equipment, checking each piece carefully and comparing competitive items, for they are not inexpensive, and it is easy to rush out and buy items that seem like a bargain at the time only to find through experience they are not what you really need or want.

Unless your interest is primarily in ceramic sculpture, you will be spending hours at the wheel. For long periods of throwing, a sit-down wheel has obvious advantages in terms of comfort over a stand-up one. For the same reasons, an electric wheel—necessarily, a variable-speed wheel that will permit sensitive control of wheel speeds—has advantages over a kick wheel. If you feel that you cannot afford an electric wheel to begin with, you can purchase a kick wheel that can be converted to an electric wheel later on. Whichever type you buy, however, avoid extremes of prices. Good kick wheels can be obtained from $100 up, but over $200 is not a good investment; the additional price will not make the wheel kick any better. For an electric wheel, you can expect to pay between $200 and $350, the higher-priced wheels usually providing greater horsepower and torque—important considerations if you think you will progress to large, heavy amounts of clay.

Your second most important investment—and the most expensive one—is a kiln. Kiln prices range from a few hundred to several thousand dollars. Since the prices are substantial, it is worthwhile to consider the advantages, at least at first, of taking your pottery elsewhere for firing. Kiln space is usually charged by the cubic inch. The cost can mount up quickly, but the chances for successful firings every time are good, and the kilns in which your pots are fired will very likely permit the more interesting glaze effects of reduction firing. The less expensive kilns are the small electric ones, in which only oxidation firing at fairly low cones is possible. Some potters manage to do very good work with these kilns, but their use is clearly limited. If you do buy one, you will find it useful for bisque firing even after you have a more expensive and versatile gas kiln, but, at the time you are making your purchases, don't forget that a small electric kiln has its limitations. It is a shame to tie up money in an inadequate kiln when you could more profitably invest in a kiln that is superior in both size and performance.

As your production increases, so does your need for space. The basement corner that served initially to house your wheel, table, and shelves will simply be too cramped to allow you the space and equipment you need now. Ideally, you will want at least as much floor space as that of a single garage, and you will want to arrange it for ease of movement and convenience.

The three separate stages of pottery making dictate to some degree the layout. In the area adjacent to the wheel, you will want the furnishings central to working the clay: shelves for storing the clay, a wedging table (two or three feet square, topped with a slab of casting plaster two or three inches thick), and ample shelves for storing greenware. Not too close to the greenware, but accessible to it, should be your electric kiln—if you have one—for bisque firing, and more shelves on which the bisque ware can be placed. The third area is the glazing area, with sufficient shelves for holding glazed pots and adequate floor space or benches for glaze buckets. A centrally located table will serve a multitude of uses. The sink should be located between the wheel and glazing areas, if possible, for it is necessary to both. And next to the sink (this is important!) must be a container for washing your clay-gummed hands and equipment before they are cleaned in the sink and for dumping clay slip and glazes. If you don't use this container, from which some of the clay can be reclaimed, the drain pipes of the sink will eventually clog with sediment. If your kiln is outside the workshop, it is well to have the glazing area near the door and as close to the kiln as possible so that you will have easy access to it.

Probably, though, you will not move directly from your hobby area to a pottery workshop. Very likely, you will just grow—like Topsy—out of one and into the other as your output increases and pottery making becomes a greater and greater part of your life.

How does that happen? How do you become a producing potter, and what do you produce? The answers, of course, depend on you, and they are not easy ones. There are, however, some important points to be considered.

The field of pottery making extends between two extremes—ceramics as a medium of sculptural art that is essentially decorative and ceramics as a medium for handcrafted, utilitarian objects. The potter interested primarily in ceramics as an art form will be alert to shows where he can enter his pieces, with the goal of establishing a reputation as an artist and of selling through galleries. His interest is in developing a distinctive technique or a type of glaze or imaginative, innovative sculptural forms. At the other extreme is the potter whose goal is to develop a line of attractive, well-crafted functional wares of the type that is fairly certain to sell to customers who enjoy the pleasure of owning and using handcrafted rather than machine-made items. As this potter's skill and speed develop and he is able to produce large numbers of pots, he becomes a production potter.

Many potters, of course, devote themselves to both pursuits, or move from one type of pottery making to the other as their circumstances change. The two extremes of directions are, in fact, less meaningful in practice than in definition, for utilitarian wares —pitchers, goblets, cups, casseroles, teapots—are often distinctive in design and decoration, and pieces that may be essentially decorative—weed pots, bottles, vases, bowls—are also to some extent functional. Furthermore, markets exist for all types of pottery that is well designed, well crafted, and aesthetically pleasing.

The markets vary from one section of the country to another, depending upon the local resurgence of interest in arts and crafts. It is safe to say, though, that the market for pottery is much greater than it was a score of years ago, or even a decade ago, and that in some parts of the country the potter is, happily, limited in sales only by the rate of his own production.

When moving into the business of selling pottery, it is best to advance slowly, gradually working up a stock of wares that gives promise of finding a market. There are many ways of discovering what types of pottery will best repay, financially, your output of time and energy.

Selling at craft fairs and art festivals is enjoyable and financially rewarding, though it is a time-consuming effort that will take you away from your studio. Fairs, festivals, and shows abound throughout the country, particularly during the summer months and before Christmas. They are sponsored by local arts and crafts guilds, recreation centers, schools, art magazines, shopping centers, chambers of commerce, individual promoters, and even neighborhood groups. To enter some, such as guilds, membership is a requirement for participation. In others, such as recreation centers, only recent or current participants in study or practice sessions may be permitted to show. Fairs organized by private promoters require a space-rental or entry fee. Some shows permit exhibitors only by invitation. Announcements of local fairs, festivals, and shows can be found in local newspapers and regional arts and crafts periodicals. The national arts and crafts publications contain announcements of some local or regional shows, but usually focus on the larger, juried shows that are open or invitational.

An advantage to beginning your commercial ventures at local weekend crafts fairs is that you have complete control over how much you want to produce for sale. If you are producing slowly, you sell only when you want to. Some potters do very nicely at this sort of activity, producing through the week and selling almost every weekend, realizing profits of a few to several thousand dollars a year. They have portable display shelves and frames on which to exhibit their wares to best advantage, and they are alert to the types of items that sell best at certain times in certain locations. They are also alert to the considerations of entrance fees and commissions to promoters. Commissions range from 10 to 25 percent of the potter's total sales, but the latter amount should be paid only when the shows are heavily advertised and have proved to be popular with the buying public. In addition to financial rewards, fairs offer the potter the opportunity to compete in a friendly manner with other craftsmen, to talk shop, to get ideas and learn, to gain exposure, and to compare pricing.

Pricing is of paramount importance. If you overprice, you don't sell; if you underprice, you are giving yourself away. Only through experience can you learn what your wares are worth on the open market. Of course, that price has little to do with what your wares are worth to you: you made them; you have an investment in them of time, energy, money, emotion, and even affection. But the buyer is looking for something to use and can hardly be expected to pay you for your emotional attachment. If you have created an object that excites your special fondness, don't try to set a monetary value on it. Simply keep the object for yourself; or, if you do sell it, take pleasure in knowing that some complete stranger is unwittingly enjoying a special bargain.

Emotion aside, pottery is generally priced according to size and use. Of the more common pottery items, cups and candle holders will normally sell for less than hanging planters, and planters will generally bring less than casseroles. Some types of wares, such as teapots, which require a considerable amount of hand work, will normally not pay as well for the time invested as larger but more easily made bowl constructions. If you are attempting to offer a reasonably complete range of wares, however, you will learn to be satisfied with less profit on some items and more on others. In the long run, the best course is to price your wares moderately so that they will move; then both you and the customer will be satisfied.

Among the visitors at crafts fairs are shop owners looking for wares they can sell in their own shops. If they see what you have, and like it, they will seek you out. You may also seek them out by taking samples of your work to show them. Normally, these dealers stock wares on consignment, giving the craftsman a share of each item sold. The dealer's share may be as low as 25 percent or as high as 40 percent; often, the arrangement is for him to receive a third of the price. Items that do not sell are returned to the craftsman, with no loss to the dealer. If you make an arrangement for placing wares on consignment, however, you should recognize that you have entered into a business agreement to supply upon demand. It is not wise to place on consignment items that you cannot produce with some readiness or that you are likely to tire of making. The dealer will hardly be pleased if you decide to stop making an item that has proved popular or if you fail to meet an agreed-upon delivery schedule.

In selecting shops in which to place consignment items, keep several things in mind. If the dealer sells mostly wholesale items or the wares of production potters (both of which he will have purchased outright and on which he may make as much as a 50 percent profit), your consignment wares (which bring less profit to the shop) will probably receive less attention by the dealer than you would like. On the other hand, if most of the inventory is consignment ware, or if there is a fairly even balance between consignment and wholesale wares, then your items are not likely to be neglected in the display or promotion. You should also have a clear understanding, preferably in writing, of how the dealer will keep track of your share of his inventory and how often you will be paid.

Selling through crafts fairs or festivals and on consignment takes its toll not only in time but in profits lost through travel or shipping expenses. These factors must be considered in pricing and in planning your delivery or selling schedule. It is advisable to restrict your deliveries to a radius of 250 miles from your studio and to plan your delivery schedule so that you can make the most economical use of your time.

Whether you are producing pottery part time or full time, you should consult a tax accountant to learn the best methods for keeping your accounts and to discuss which of your expenses are tax deductions. In addition to the direct cost of your supplies and the depreciation of equipment, such expenses as mailing your wares, traveling to fairs, festivals, and shops, and general overhead (utilities, estimated or actual rent for studio, etc.) are all very likely deductible.

Another major consideration is the seasonal aspect of the market for pottery. The Christmas season of gift giving may well account for a third or more of your annual sales. It is thus necessary either to have a stock of wares that can be ready for the Christmas season or to be able to produce rapidly beginning in September, when shops start planning and stocking for Christmas. In either case, sources of supplies and firing must be dependable and on a guaranteed schedule. If the shops through which you sell are dependent on either summer or winter tourists, the same preplanning of your production will be necessary for the periods preceding the tourist seasons.

Pottery making can bring you a pleasant supplementary income and even a comfortable livelihood if you become sufficiently skilled to produce good wares quickly and do not expect huge profits. Not that large profits are impossible. Many potters cannot keep up with their orders, and some, in areas of the country where tourism and crafts sales are high, gross between $20,000 and $25,000 annually.

Pottery does not, however, sell itself. If you plan to make a living through pottery, you must know the basis of good business management and simple bookkeeping, and you would do well to be reasonably aggressive in getting your wares before the public. Good pots sitting on the shelves in your studio will collect only dust, not profits.

Since the varied aspects of pottery making and selling are very time consuming, some husbands and wives combine their abilities and work as teams, one person doing the production, the other handling the sales. On the other hand, single potters can place their wares in the hands of a representative who will handle the business aspects on a commission basis. Another possibility, if you are attracted to the idea of having a business of your own, is to open your own pottery shop.

MANAGING A POTTERY SHOP AND STUDIO

Opening a retail pottery shop is vastly different from establishing yourself as a selling potter. Some potters prefer to maintain their independence from business concerns as much as possible and remain their own taskmasters in their studios. Other potters, however, are much attracted to the idea of operating a shop. They enjoy the spirit of the business world; perhaps they have an interest in pottery and crafts but not the skill necessary to become exceptional potters; maybe they prefer to sell their own work through their own stores.

There are a number of ways in which a pottery shop can be set up. If you are a working potter and want to sell your own pottery, the least complex type of shop is a working studio with a separate sales area. This is a particularly good arrangement for a husband and wife team, with one person handling the sales while the other produces pottery. If the potter tries to handle both tasks, either the production or the business is likely to suffer. This difficulty can be overcome, however, by having the sales area open only during specified hours on certain days, when the potter can give full attention to sales.

The producing potter may also establish an apprentice program, whereby promising potters exchange a fixed number of hours of work in the shop or studio for the use of the studio equipment and the opportunity to learn more about pottery making. In this way, everyone—owner and apprentices alike—gets pots made, and the sales area is manned at all times.

Fig. 250. Section of production workshop area shared by potter and apprentices. Movement in the workshop is from front to rear. Pots are thrown in the front, stored in the middle, and glazed and fired in the back of the workshop. The kiln room houses an 8-cubic-foot electric kiln for bisque firing and a 21-cubic-foot gas kiln for glaze firing.

Other arrangements are also workable. A group of potters may establish a cooperative shop, sharing equally in the management and the production, and either do their potting in the studio area or at another location. Or a person interested in selling pottery but not particularly involved in production can operate a pottery or a crafts shop, taking work on consignment or purchasing it wholesale. Variations and combinations of these arrangements are all possible, depending on the interests and abilities of the persons involved.

The sales area may, in fact, be only an adjunct to the central concern of a group of potters who set up their own pottery—in this sense, a place where pottery is made—in order to produce wares to place on consignment or sell wholesale to other shops as well as through their own. The workshop may not even be in a location where sales are practicable. A barn or warehouse in an out of the way place, where rent is low and space expansive, is an ideal site for a pottery.

A workshop shared by several potters on a cooperative basis, or by a potter-owner and apprentice potters, must be large enough to give ample working space to each person. The large workshop layout is governed by the same considerations as the smaller workshop, though the increased amount of work produced in the shop will require more wheels and larger kilns and even further types of equipment, such as a slab roller and a pug mill. The advantage of having several potters work together is that they can pool their resources for kilns and other equipment in the workshop operation.

It is important to have a good location for your shop. Otherwise, even the best pottery will sit undisturbed on the shelves. Good choices for locations are small, specialty shopping areas with quality shops featuring various arts and crafts and imported,

Fig. 251. Production pottery area showing newly finished goblets drying upside down near the wheel area where they were trimmed and assembled.

interesting wares. Such arts and crafts centers have been and are being developed throughout the country, often in areas with heavy tourist or sight-seeing traffic. Many cities have "old town" areas, where old buildings have been renovated to suggest something of the quality of life during earlier, less hectic times. Some small towns with nearby sites of historical interest or scenic attraction exist principally as arts and crafts centers. Such locations are ideal, for customers are generally relaxed and unhurried, interested in looking, and willing to buy. The pottery shop must, of course, fit in with surrounding shops if it is to attract the clientele drawn to the shopping area. A woman customer on the way to a supermarket is hardly likely to be concerned with pottery at that time, whereas if she is out looking at jewelry or shopping at a boutique or lunching at a quaint restaurant, she is more probably in the mood to look at, and to buy, crafts items.

Other considerations worth serious thought are the extent of available close parking—an absolute necessity—and rent. With rent figured on either a flat rate or a percentage, you will be protected through the slow months—and there will be slow months. Avoid a combination of minimum rent plus a percentage of the sales, whereby you pay more if you make more but must still meet the minimum during the slack periods. Pottery sales do not permit high markups, and the rental arrangement can be the deciding factor between profit and loss.

If the shop is to be combined with a production area in a commercial zone, it is necessary to check out ordinances involving the use of kilns. You must also have your landlord's written approval regarding the locations of your kilns. What provisions are there for kiln space? Who pays for installation?

The size of the shop is determined by its type and by the anticipated volume of business. A working

Fig. 252. A corner of the sales area in the shop of Frank Howell. Located in a shopping complex featuring rustic motifs, the shop is furnished in barnwood and redwood that provide an appropriate setting for the display of hand-crafted pottery. The pots shown here and in Fig. 253 were made by several professional potters and apprentices.

shop needs almost twice as much space as a strictly retail shop. A sales area of from 300 to 600 square feet can stock a very large range of wares, but an effective and economical use of shelves and racks for hanging items can facilitate the attractive display of pottery in much smaller space. In a working shop, with a recommended floor space of about 1,000 square feet, it is essential to set off the production area from the sales area. Customers like to watch pottery being made, but railings or waist-high dividers should keep your unfinished pots at a safe distance from curious fingers and inquisitive children.

Fortunately, handcrafted ware lends itself to effective display on rustic, handmade shelving that most persons can build themselves. Natural wood, new or aged, works exceptionally well. Barnwood, common rough-finished redwood, and used timbers such as those shown in Figs. 252 and 253 provide both strength and the appropriate background for pottery.

Because of public concern with the danger of lead in glazes, you should be sure to use lead-free glazes for all pottery intended for food use. Also label the pots or put placards on the shelves explaining that your pottery is safe for use with food, even acidic foods such as coffee, orange juice, and wine. You should also warn customers not to place pottery directly over an open flame or heating element and (to guard completely against breakage) place pottery dishes in a cold oven and then heat the oven to the desired temperature. Assure customers that all pottery can be placed in a dishwasher.

The pottery itself should not only be as good as you can get, but also sufficiently varied in style, type, and price to attract a wide range of tastes. As a rule, the more pots you have, the more you will sell. If you cannot supply all the types yourself, advertisements in newspapers and art periodicals, on college bulletin boards, and at supply stores will attract potters willing to place their pots on consignment. But be selective and cautious in making consignment arrangements. The reputation of your shop begins early, and you will want not only good wares but reliable, dependable potters. Probably, they will be able to supply the shop with items you don't like to make yourself. Not everyone enjoys throwing mugs or making teapots. Build up a dependable supply of staple items, but allow as well for seasonal differences. A local Octoberfest may well result in a run on beer steins. Winter may bring a demand for casseroles, soup tureens and mugs, and large coffee mugs. The return of warm weather will bring an increased demand for wine goblets and planters.

Try to offer a variety of glaze types. Some customers will prefer the brilliancy of gloss glazes; some will like the dull matte finishes. Make certain you have a number of price brackets, with the majority of the items under twenty dollars. If traffic is good, you will do well with items under five dollars—coffee mugs, goblets, candle holders. The small sales add up nicely. Time quickly shows you which items move. Also, don't let your inventory become stale—steady customers always enjoy new and varied items.

An occasional customer comes in knowing exactly what he wants—a casserole, for example, with a particular type of decoration, a special glaze effect, or a style you don't regularly stock. Be wary of working on special orders unless the item called for is one that you feel comfortable making. It is better to recommend a potter who does work of the type the customer wants rather than take time from your regular production to do a special order not in your own style. On the other hand, if several customers ask for the same item or type of ware, it will clearly be to your advantage to try stocking it.

Pottery sales—in fact, all crafts sales—are seasonal. During the slow months and the good months sales may differ as much as eight times in volume. It is necessary to plan ahead—to anticipate both volume and types of sales. It may also be necessary to supplement the slow months by dealing in supplies and equipment for potters. You may wish to become a dealer for pottery-making equipment—wheels and kilns—and order them as customers want them, while keeping a stock of smaller craft tools. Until you have grown in experience and know what to anticipate in the way of sales, it is best to keep only a small inventory of these items and absolutely essential to have a clear understanding regarding discounts (you will want at least a 25 percent markup), guarantees, and returns. Make sure you test or check out any item thoroughly before offering it for sale.

As mentioned before, the profit on pottery is not high. You should guard against high overhead items —salaried employees, expensive furnishings, elaborate and costly display shelves and racks. But you will need to advertise—through business cards, newspaper ads, radio spot commercials, posters, etc. An annual open house to which you send invitations to established customers and potential ones can be an excellent promotional venture. Good wares, a good location, and a good reputation are the best guarantees of good sales, however, and the best advertising cannot compensate for deficiencies in these areas.

The resurgence in crafts sales can be variously accounted for—nostalgia for the nontechnological past, a general affluence, and more leisure time for browsing and shopping. These conditions are not likely to change quickly, and as long as people have an interest in handcrafted goods at prices that are competitive with mass-produced wares, there are comfortable, enjoyable livings to be made through pottery.

Fig. 253. A pottery display arrangement by uses and types permits the customer to see the varied styles of the different potters whose wares are shown. Label cards and posters identify types and provide information about the pottery—for example, that the glazes are lead-free and safe for cooking and table use.

Glossary of Pottery Terms

Absorbency. The characteristic of clay that permits it to soak in water. See *Porosity.*

Appliqué. The decorating technique of affixing clay pieces to wet or leatherhard clay.

Ball mill. A porcelain jar in which porcelain balls are used for finely grinding wet or dry glaze chemicals. The jar is turned mechanically to achieve the grinding action.

Banding. The decorative technique of brushing glaze or slip on a pot as it rotates on a wheel.

Banding wheel. See *Modeling wheel.*

Bat. A slab of casting plaster, particle board, or other material used as an extension of the wheel head, or for working hand-built pots.

Biscuit. See *Bisque.*

Bisque. Clay ware that has undergone a low-temperature firing prior to glazing.

Bisque firing. First firing of clay, usually between 1600 and 1850 degrees F., as a step toward preparing it for glaze decoration and firing.

Blowing. Breaking or bursting of pottery during the firing, resulting from heating the kiln too quickly to permit steam inside of clay to escape.

Bone china. A translucent chinaware made from clay containing a great amount of bone ash.

Carbonates. Metallic substances used as glaze and engobe colorants.

Carving. The decorating technique of cutting into leatherhard clay.

Casting. The forming technique of pouring clay slip into hollow plaster molds.

Centering. Process of forcing a lump of clay into a perfectly symmetrical mound at the center of the wheel head.

Ceramics. The art or technique of making hard, heat-resistant objects by firing clay or other minerals; also the objects made using this technique.

China clay. See *Kaolin.*

Chuck. A cylinder of plastic, fired clay, or plaster used to hold a bottle when it is trimmed on a wheel head.

Clay. A type of soil, consisting mainly of decomposed granite in combination with organic and inorganic impurities, which forms a wet paste and hardens when heated.

Clay body. A compounded mixture of different clays.

Coil. A piece of clay rolled into a ropelike shape.

Coiling. The shaping technique of using clay coils in an upward spiral to build the walls of a pot.

Collaring. The technique of narrowing the top or neck of a pot by squeezing the clay inward with the hands.

Colorants. Usually metallic oxides added to a colorless base glaze to achieve color.

Cones. See *Pyrometric cones.*

Crawling. The beading up of a glaze on the surface of a pot.

Crazing. A glaze condition characterized by a fine network of cracks and resulting when the glaze contracts more rapidly than the clay during cooling.

Damp box. A lined box used for keeping unfinished clay objects moist and plastic.

Decalcomania. The decorative technique of using transfer paper to apply glaze designs to pottery.

Deflocculant. A compound used in a glaze or slip to reduce the amount of water necessary and allow the clay particles to exist in proper suspension without "flocking" together.

Earthenware clay. A clay with a high content of iron impurities that fires at temperatures usually under 2000 degrees F.

Elephant ear sponge. Finely grained sponge used for finishing pottery.

Engobe. A colored slip used for decorating.

Fettling knife. A knife with thin, flexible steel blade used for cutting and carving.

Finishing. The process of smoothing the surfaces and rims of pots in the greenware or leatherhard stage.

Finishing rubber. Rubber palette used for smoothing clay surfaces.

Firing. The process of subjecting pots to intense heat in a furnace or kiln. See *Bisque firing* and *Glaze firing.*

Firing cone. The pyrometric cone used to indicate when the desired firing temperature has been reached.

Flux. Low-melting compound added to a glaze to reduce the melting temperature of the higher-melting compounds.

Foot. A ring cut into, or mounted on, the base of a pot.

Glaze. A glasslike surface achieved by coating pottery with minerals in liquid suspension and firing it until the minerals melt together and fuse with the pottery.

Glaze firing. The second firing of clay, after it has been bisque fired and glazed, at a temperature high enough to melt the glaze and fuse it to the pot.

Greenware. Pottery before it has been fired, in the plastic, leatherhard, or air-dried stage.

Grog. Ground or powdered fired clay, added to clay mixes to give strength and reduce shrinkage.

Guard cone. The pyrometric cone used to indicate whether the firing has gone beyond the desired temperature. Usually one cone higher than the firing cone.

Guide cone. The pyrometric cone used to indicate that the desired firing temperature has nearly been reached. Usually one cone lower than the firing cone. Also called "warning cone."

Head. The disk on a potter's wheel where clay is centered and thrown.

Incising. The decorating technique of scratching clay.

Jiggering. A production technique for flat pottery involving the use of a mold on the wheel head and a profile tool or template for achieving the desired bottom contour.

Kaolin. Pure clay, used for compounding glazes and porcelain. Also called "china clay."

Kick wheel. A potter's wheel on which the potter turns with his foot a platform connected by a shaft to the wheel head, thereby turning the wheel head.

Kiln. A furnace constructed of firebrick capable of withstanding high temperatures and used for firing pottery.

Kiln furniture. Shelves, shelf supports, and stilts used for stacking wares to be fired in the kiln.

Kiln wash. A coating of kaolin and flint used to protect the kiln bottom and shelves from damage by glazes.

Leatherhard. A term used to describe the condition of clay when it has dried to the stage where it can no longer be shaped but is still soft enough to be carved and scored.

Lifting. The process of pulling up clay on a wheel head to form walls that can be shaped into a pot. Also called "pulling up."

Loop tool. Any of a variety of tools with ribbon steel loops at one or both ends, used for trimming and carving.

Maturity. The temperature at which a clay or glaze fuses and reaches its full development.

Modeling tool. Any of a variety of steel, wood, or bone tools used for trimming and carving.

Modeling wheel. Rotating wheel head mounted on a base, used for hand-building and decorating. Also called "banding wheel."

Needle. Handle-mounted needle used for cutting, scoring, and measuring clay wall thickness.

Nylon clay cutter. Nylon cord, sometimes tied at both ends to small wooden pieces, used for cutting clay.

Opening. Process of making a depression or hole in the middle of a mound of centered clay on the wheel head and then pulling clay across to one side so that it can be lifted and shaped.

Overglaze. A glaze applied over another glaze in either the raw or fired state.

Oxidation firing. A firing in which the mixture of air and fuel allows for the complete combustion of the fuel.

Oxides. Metallic substances used as coloring agents in glazes, engobes, and clay slips.

Paddling. A shaping technique using a paddle to flatten the sides of a piece of pottery.

Pinching. A method of hand-building and a decorative technique involving the use of only the fingers and hands as tools.

Pinholes. Minute holes in the surface of a glaze.

Plasticity. The characteristic of a clay that permits it to retain its shape as it is being formed by the potter.

Porcelain. A clay that fires to very hard nonporous pottery at temperatures up to about 2491 degrees F.

Porosity. The characteristic of clay or fired ware that permits it to retain water. See *Absorbency.*

Pot. General term for any piece of pottery made by a potter.

Potter's knife. Knife with double-edged, pointed blade used for cutting and carving.

Potter's wheel. A foot-powered or motor-driven machine designed to turn clay on a wheel head so that the potter can shape it.

Pottery. Pots; also, a factory or workshop where pottery is produced.

Primary clay. Clay that is found in its place of origin. Also called "residual clay."

Pugging. Process of mixing clay thoroughly with a pug mill.

Pug mill. A machine consisting of a large screw-type blade (as in a meat grinder), which works the clay against metal baffles to produce an even consistency.

Pulling up. See *Lifting.*

Pyrometric cones. Three-sided pyramids of clay and glaze designed to melt or deform at designated temperatures and used to indicate the temperature within the kiln during firing.

Raku. A low-fire firing process using heavily grogged clay.

Reduction firing. A firing in which the oxygen in the air of the firing chamber is reduced so that the resulting free carbon will combine with the oxygen in the clay or the glaze and create a chemical change in it.

Removing. Process of removing a pot from the wheel head after it has been thrown.

Residual clay. See *Primary clay.*

Ribs. Wooden, steel, or bone palettes used for finishing clay surfaces.

Scoring. Technique of roughening pieces of clay with a sharp object such as a needle prior to joining.

Secondary clay. Clay that has been moved by the forces of nature from its place of origin. Also called "sedimentary clay."

Sedimentary clay. See *Secondary clay.*

Sgraffito. The decorative technique of scratching through slip to expose the clay underneath it.

Shaping. Process of forming clay into a pot or sculptured form.

Shattering. Breaking of a pot as a result of excessive compression or shivering of the glaze. See *Shivering.*

Shivering. A glaze flaw resulting when the glaze contracts more slowly than the clay during the cooling period, causing the glaze to break away in slivers from the clay.

Slab. A rolled-out piece of clay; a method of handbuilding using clay slabs.

Slip. Clay in water suspension.

Slurry. A thick mixture of water and clay particles. See *Slip.*

Stamping. The decorative technique of pressing designs into wet clay.

Stoneware clay. A clay that fires to hard, dense pottery at temperatures from about 2185 to 2381 degrees F.

Terra cotta. Literally "baked earth"; the term generally refers to a combination of red and white clays that have been fired but not glazed.

Throwing. The technique of making pottery on a potter's wheel.

Throwing off the head. Technique of making pottery from clay placed either directly on the wheel head or on a bat affixed to the wheel head.

Throwing off the hump. See *Throwing off the mound.*

Throwing off the mound. Technique of making pottery from the top portion of a large mound of clay centered on the wheel head. Also called "throwing off the hump."

Throwing stick. Tool used for the inside shaping of tall pots.

Trimming. The process of cutting away irregularities and excess clay trimming from the walls and base and of forming a foot on a pot; the final step of throwing a pot. Also called "turning."

Turning. See *Trimming.*

Turning tool. Metal tool with a teardrop or triangular head, used for trimming at the base of a pot either on the wheel or at the leatherhard stage.

Vitrification. The point at which clay particles fuse and glaze becomes glasslike because of intense heat.

Warning cone. See *Guard cone.*

Water smoking. The early period of firing when the atmospheric water in raw clay is driven off.

Wax resist. A wax applied to the base or other area of a pot to keep it free of glaze, engobes, or oxides; the decorative technique employing wax.

Wedging. The process of forcibly kneading the clay in order to remove air from it and to condition it for use in making pottery.

Wedging board. Plaster-filled box or table top used as an absorbent surface for wedging clay.

Wheel. See *Potter's wheel.*

Wood knife. Any wooden potter's or sculpture knife used for trimming or shaping a pot while still on the wheel.

Suggested Reading

The following brief list of books may be supplemented by *Bibliography: Clay,* a 1972 reference guide prepared by the Research & Education Department of the American Crafts Council, 44 West 53rd Street, New York, N.Y. 10019.

Instructional Texts

Ball, F. Carlton. *Decorating Pottery.* Columbus, Ohio: Ceramics Monthly. Explains basic methods of decorating pottery with clay, slip, and glaze.

———, and Janice Lovoos. *Making Pottery Without a Wheel.* New York: Van Nostrand Reinhold, 1965. Covers all phases of hand-building techniques and decoration.

Behrens, Richard. *Glaze Projects.* Columbus, Ohio: Ceramics Monthly. Provides formulas for numerous lead-free glazes in all firing ranges.

Berensohn, Paulus. *Finding One's Way with Clay: Pinched Pottery and the Color of Clay.* New York: Simon and Schuster, 1972. The art and technique of pinched pottery as a means of self-expression.

Cardew, Michael. *Pioneer Pottery.* London: Longmans, 1971. Covers all phases of pottery making from digging the clay to the finished product.

Conrad, John. *Ceramic Formulas: The Complete Compendium.* New York: Macmillan, 1973. Glaze formulas for all firing ranges.

Green, David. *Pottery Glazes.* New York: Watson-Guptill, 1973. An introduction to pottery glazes, with useful reference tables.

Hetherington, A. L. *Chinese Ceramic Glazes.* London: Commonwealth Press, 1948. An authoritative study of iron and copper glazes.

Kenny, John B. *Ceramic Sculpture: Methods and Processes.* Philadelphia: Chilton, 1953. Explains all phases of ceramic sculpture from beginning to advanced projects.

Leach, Bernard. *A Potter's Book.* Levittown, New York: Transatlantic Arts, 1951. The first study of the Korean and Japanese potters' traditions, beginning with the Sung dynasty.

Nelson, Glenn. *Ceramics: A Potter's Handbook.* Third Edition. New York: Holt, Rinehart and Winston, 1971. A comprehensive book on all aspects of ceramics by a notable authority.

Norton, F. H. *Fine Ceramics: Technology and Applications.* New York: McGraw-Hill, 1970. Thorough technical discussion of the general principles involved in the commercial manufacture of fine ceramics.

Parmalee, Cullen W. *Ceramic Glazes.* Boston: Colners, 1968. A study of glazes from raw materials to batch recipes.

Priolo, Joan B. *Ceramics—and How to Decorate Them.* New York: Sterling, 1958. Describes numerous decorating techniques, with useful illustrations.

Rhodes, Daniel. *Clay and Glazes for the Potter.* Revised Edition. Philadelphia: Chilton, 1957. A comprehensive book on clays, glaze ingredients and calculations, and firing techniques.

———. *Kilns: Design, Construction, and Operation.* Radnor, Pa.: Chilton, 1968. Explains various types of kilns, including their history, operation, and construction.

———. *Stoneware and Porcelain: The Art of High-Fired Pottery.* Philadelphia: Chilton, 1959. An authoritative volume on the traditions, techniques, and materials used in high-fired pottery.

Riegger, Hal. *Raku: Art and Techniques.* New York: Van Nostrand Reinhold, 1970. A complete book on Raku.

Rottger, Ernst. *Creative Clay Design.* New York: Van Nostrand Reinhold, 1972. A useful photographic approach to design, from basic to elaborate shapes.

Sellers, Thomas. *Ceramic Projects.* Columbus, Ohio: Ceramics Monthly. A manual describing numerous projects from basic forms to fountains and jewelry.

Pottery History

Cox, Warren E. *The Book of Pottery and Porcelain.* 2 volumes. New York: Crown, 1970. A profusely illustrated study for the craftsman, collector, and student.

Design Quarterly, Numbers 42–43, 1958. Black-and-white photographs of works of leading contemporary potters, with biographies of the artists and their own statements of their aesthetic intentions.

Foley, Suzanne. *A Decade of Ceramic Art 1962–1972.* San Francisco: San Francisco Museum of Art, 1972. Catalog of an exhibition documenting the development of contemporary American ceramic art.

Henzke, Lucile. *American Art Pottery.* Camden, N.J.: Thomas Nelson, 1970. Emphasizes hand-decorated and hand-modeled pottery "as opposed to porcelain or just plain crockery."

Honey, W. B., editor. *The Faber Monographs on Pottery and Porcelain.* London: Faber and Faber. Authoritative volumes including:
  Charleston, R. J. *Roman Pottery*
  Garner, F. H. *English Delftware*
  Honey, W. B. *Wedgwood Ware*
  Jenyns, Soame. *Later Chinese Porcelain*
  ———. *Ming Pottery and Porcelain*
  Lane, Arthur. *French Faïence*
  ———. *Greek Pottery*
  ———. *Italian Porcelain*

Lewenstein, Eileen, and Emmanuel Cooper, editors. *New Ceramics.* New York: Van Nostrand Reinhold, 1974. Photographic survey of trends in contemporary pottery throughout the world.

Ramsay, John. *American Potters and Pottery.* Clinton, Mass.: Hale, Cushman & Flint, 1939. A history of American pottery from the standpoint of the collector, well illustrated with both photographs and drawings.

Sanders, Herbert, with the collaboration of Kenkichi Tomimoto. *The World of Japanese Ceramics.* Tokyo and Palo Alto, Calif.: Kodansha International, 1967. An authoritative study of modern and historical Japanese ceramic techniques.

Savage, George. *Porcelain Through the Ages.* Cranbury, N.J.: A. S. Barnes, 1961. A companion volume to *Pottery Through the Ages.*

————. *Pottery Through the Ages.* Harmondsworth, Middlesex: Penguin Books, 1959. A "bird's-eye view" of the history of earthenware and stoneware.

————, and Harold Newman. *An Illustrated Dictionary of Ceramics.* New York: Van Nostrand Reinhold, 1974. Definitions of over 3,000 terms relating to all aspects of ceramics from antiquity to the present day.

Stiles, Helen E. *Pottery of the Europeans.* New York: Dutton, 1940. Emphasizes "the historical and social significance of pottery—its use and its art."

Walters, H. B. *History of Ancient Pottery.* 2 volumes. London: John Murray, 1905. A copiously illustrated treatise on Greek, Etruscan, and Roman pottery, based on Samuel Birch's 1858 book of the same title.

Wykes-Joyce, Max. *7000 Years of Pottery and Porcelain.* New York: Philosophical Library, 1958. The history of pottery as "the history of Man."

Index

The Authors

FRANK HOWELL has been a potter-teacher in California for the past ten years. He studied under Maurice Grossman at the University of Arizona, where he received his B.F.A. degree. He also has an M.F.A. degree in sculpture from the University of Oregon, where he taught elementary sculpture. While working for an art credential in Los Angeles, he headed the ceramics program for South Pasadena, teaching hand-building pottery techniques to children, teens, and adults. He taught ceramics in the Los Angeles city schools for five years, developing new programs on both the high school and adult education levels. In 1968 Mr. Howell organized and equipped a special adult ceramics program in a Los Angeles minority area; this was the first program in the city high schools to use the materials and techniques of a professional potter's studio. Since 1971 he has operated his own shop and pottery in Old Town, Los Gatos, California, where he holds pottery classes and sells his own work and that of local potters. Mr. Howell has exhibited in numerous shows, including the Cerritos Ceramics Annual; the San Diego Expo, where he won an award for ceramics; the Los Angeles County Fair; the American Craftsman Council Show; and others. His work in sculpture and pottery is in private collections throughout the United States. He has completed two large steel and concrete play sculptures for parks in South Pasadena and Montebello, California.